27.20

New Common Entrance Mathematics

Second Edition

Also available from Stanley Thornes:

Layne et al *ST(P) Caribbean Mathematics 1*
Layne et al *ST(P) Caribbean Mathematics 2*
Layne et al *ST(P) Caribbean Mathematics 3*
Greer and Layne, *Certificate Mathematics – A Revision Course for the Caribbean*
Greer and Layne, *CXC Basic Mathematics – A Revision Course*

New Common Entrance Mathematics

Second Edition

Walter Phillips BA
Head of Mathematics
St. Lucy Secondary School, Barbados

Stanley Thornes (Publishers) Ltd

First published in 1986 by:
Stanley Thornes (Publishers) Ltd
Delta Place
27 Bath Road
CHEL TENHAM
GL53 7TH
United Kingdom
Second Edition 1994

02   03   04   05   /   10

A catalogue record of this book is available from the British Library.

ISBN 0-7487-1761-7

Typeset by Tech-Set, Gateshead, Tyne & Wear
Printed and bound in China by Midas.

Contents

	Preface	viii
	Acknowledgements	viii
Chapter 1	**Number Patterns**	1
	Series and patterns. Magic squares.	
Chapter 2	**Notation and Numeration**	6
	Reading numbers. Writing numbers in figures. Expansion of numbers.	
Chapter 3	**Computation of Whole Numbers**	12
	Addition of whole numbers. Subtraction of whole numbers. Multiplication by one-digit numbers. Multiplication by 10, 100, 1000 and multiples of these. Multiplication by two- and three-digit numbers. Division by one-digit numbers. Long division. Using multiplication and division facts. Order of operation. Problems involving more than one operation.	
Chapter 4	**Using the Signs $+$, $-$, $\times$, $\div$, $<$, $=$, $>$**	29
Chapter 5	**Factors and Multiples**	32
	Factors. Prime factors. Expressing a number as a product of prime factors. Multiples. Lowest common multiple (L.C.M.)	
Chapter 6	**Some Sets of Numbers**	37
	Whole numbers. Natural numbers. Even numbers. Odd numbers. Prime numbers.	
Chapter 7	**Fractions**	44
	Equivalent fractions. Cancelling. Mixed numbers and improper fractions. Addition and subtraction of fractions. Multiplication of fractions. Finding a fraction of a number, money, time, mass, etc. Division of fractions. Mixed $+$, $-$, $\times$, $\div$ and 'of', of fractions. Problems involving fractions. Ordering fractions.	
Chapter 8	**Decimals**	61
	Place value. Writing decimals as fractions or mixed numbers. Writing fractions or mixed numbers as decimals. Writing vulgar fractions as decimals. Addition and subtraction of decimals. Multiplication of decimals. Division of decimals. Ordering decimals.	

Chapter 9 Percentages 74

Changing fractions to percentages. Changing percentages to fractions in their lowest terms. Finding a percentage of a number, money, mass, length, etc. Problems involving percentages. Profit and loss. Discount. Miscellaneous problems.

Chapter 10 Angles 85

Right angles. Acute angles. Straight angles. Obtuse angles. Reflex angles. The circle. Calculations based on the right angle. Calculations based on the straight angle. Calculations based on the circle.

Chapter 11 Plane Figures 95

Triangles. The square and the rectangle. The parallelogram. The rhombus. The trapezium. The circle.

Chapter 12 Solid Figures 102

The cuboid. The cube. The cylinder. The cone. The sphere.

Chapter 13 Lines of Symmetry 109

Chapter 14 Squares and Square Roots 114

Chapter 15 Indices 117

Chapter 16 Bases Other Than 10 119

Changing other bases to base 10. Changing base 10 numbers to other bases.

Chapter 17 Substitution 124

Chapter 18 Metric Units 126

Units of length. Units of mass. Capacity.

Chapter 19 Measurement 134

Perimeter of closed figures. Area of irregular shapes. Area of rectangles and squares. Area of borders and shaded parts of squares and rectangles. Area of triangles. Volume. Time. 24-hour clock. The calendar. Money. Foreign money.

Chapter 20 Coordinates 169

Naming points.

Chapter 21 Averages 174

Chapter 22 Unitary Method 177

Chapter 23 Ratio 179

Meaning of ratio. Dividing into a given ratio. Dividing or sharing so that one part is x times another. Dividing so that one part is more than or less than the other.

Chapter 24 Equations 183

Chapter 25 Sets   189
Union of sets. Intersection of sets. Problems based on Venn diagrams.

Chapter 26 **Distance, Speed and Time**   195
Meaning of metres per second and kilometres per hour. Problems involving distance, speed and time.

Chapter 27 **Graphs**   198
The pictograph. The line graph. The bar chart. The pie chart.

Chapter 28

Scale Drawing   207

Revision Exercises   211

Preface

New Common Entrance Mathematics covers all the topics included in the Primary Mathematics syllabus. It is designed, along with the accompanying Workbook, to prepare pupils for the Common Entrance Examination. However, it will also be helpful to lessable pupils who are in the early stages of the secondary school course.

Some of the topics which are included will be new to the pupils; the teacher should therefore begin with these. The remaining topics will have been covered earlier in normal class work, and all these will be revised during school time in preparation for the examination.

The Workbook forms an integral part of the course. In addition a separate volume of Teacher's Notes and Answers relevant to the Textbook and Workbook is available. This book is expressly designed to help and guide the teachers in checking and correcting the pupil's work, and should be used only by teachers and not by pupils.

Walter Phillips
1994

Acknowledgements

I would like to express my thanks to all the staff at Stanley Thornes Publishers who have given their best professional assistance in getting the work into finished form.

Chapter One

Number Patterns

A. Series and patterns

Look at the following three series:

(1)	5,	10,	15,	20,	25
(2)	4,	5,	7,	10,	14
(3)	2,	4,	8,	16,	32

Notice that each successive number is bigger than the one before it. To make a number bigger, we either add a positive number to it or multiply it by a positive number.

In **(1)** we get each successive number by adding 5.
In **(2)** we get each successive number by adding 1, 2, 3, 4.
In **(3)** we get each successive number by multiplying by 2.

Look at the following three series:

(a)	40,	36,	32,	28,	24
(b)	31,	30,	27,	22,	15
(c)	100,	10,	1,	$\frac{1}{10}$,	$\frac{1}{100}$

Notice that each successive number is smaller than the one before it. To make a number smaller, we either subtract a positive number from it or divide it by a positive number greater than one.

In **(a)** we get each successive number by subtracting 4.
In **(b)** we get each successive number by subtracting 1, 3, 5, 7 (odd numbers).
In **(c)** we get each successive number by dividing by 10.

Exercise 1 Write the next two numbers in each of the following series:

1.	2,	4,	6,	8,	...,	...
2.	3,	6,	9,	12,	...,	...
3.	1,	7,	13,	19,	...,	...
4.	8,	16,	24,	32,	...,	...
5.	10,	21,	32,	43,	...,	...
6.	2,	3,	5,	8,	...,	...
7.	50,	100,	150,	200,	...,	...
8.	2.02,	2.04,	2.06,	2.08,	...,	...
9.	1.50,	1.75,	2.00,	2.25,	...,	...
10.	1,	4,	9,	16,	...,	...
11.	1,	2,	4,	8,	...,	...
12.	12,	23,	34,	45,	...,	...
13.	3,	6,	12,	24,	...,	...
14.	1,	2,	4,	5,	7,	..., ...
15.	1,	$2\frac{1}{2}$,	4,	$5\frac{1}{2}$,	...,	...

Exercise 2 Write the next two numbers in each of the following series:

1.	20,	19,	18,	17,	...,	...
2.	36,	33,	30,	27,	...,	...
3.	50,	45,	40,	35,	...,	...
4.	60,	52,	44,	36,	...,	...
5.	75,	65,	55,	45,	...,	...
6.	25,	24,	22,	19,	...,	...
7.	64,	32,	16,	8,	...,	...
8.	81,	27,	9,	3,	...,	...
9.	1.06,	1.04,	1.02,	1.00,	...,	...
10.	87,	76,	65,	54,	...,	...
11.	7,	$6\frac{1}{2}$,	6,	$5\frac{1}{2}$,	...,	...
12.	49,	36,	25,	16,	...,	...
13.	1000,	100,	10,	1,	...,	...
14.	40,	38,	34,	28,	...,	...
15.	40,	39,	37,	36,	34,	..., ...

Exercise 3   Write the missing number in each of the following series:

1.	1,	3,	5,	. . . ,	9
2.	4,	8,	12,	. . . ,	20
3.	6,	12,	. . . ,	24,	30
4.	10,	20,	30,	. . . ,	50
5.	2,	4,	8,	16,	. . .
6.	45,	44,	43,	42,	. . .
7.	7,	14,	21,	28,	. . .
8.	50,	48,	46,	44,	. . .
9.	1,	3,	9,	27,	. . .
10.	5,	6,	8,	11,	. . .
11.	40,	37,	34,	. . . ,	28
12.	1,	2,	4,	7,	. . .
13.	0.24,	0.26,	0.28,	. . . ,	0.32
14.	100,	81,	64,	49,	. . .
15.	2,	3,	6,	11,	18,	. . .
16.	1,	3,	7,	13,	21,	. . .
17.	30,	29,	27,	24,	. . . ,	15
18.	8,	$7\frac{1}{2}$,	7,	$6\frac{1}{2}$,	. . .
19.	8,	4,	2,	1,	. . .
20.	$\dfrac{1 \times 2}{2}$,	$\dfrac{2 \times 3}{3}$,	$\dfrac{3 \times 4}{4}$,	$\dfrac{4 \times 5}{5}$,	. . .

Exercise 4   Write the next line in each of the following:

1.
$$1 = 1 \times 1$$
$$1 + 3 = 2 \times 2$$
$$1 + 3 + 5 = 3 \times 3$$
$$\ldots = \ldots$$

2.
$$2 = 1 \times 2$$
$$2 + 4 = 2 \times 3$$
$$2 + 4 + 6 = 3 \times 4$$
$$\ldots = \ldots$$

3.
$$3 \times 37 = 111$$
$$6 \times 37 = 222$$
$$9 \times 37 = 333$$
$$\ldots = \ldots$$

4.
$$9 \times 9 + 7 = 88$$
$$98 \times 9 + 6 = 888$$
$$987 \times 9 + 5 = 8888$$
$$\ldots = \ldots$$

5. $1 \times 9 + 2 = 11$

$12 \times 9 + 3 = 111$

$123 \times 9 + 4 = 1111$

$\ldots \qquad = \ldots$

7. $7 \times 15\,873 = 111\,111$

$14 \times 15\,873 = 222\,222$

$21 \times 15\,873 = 333\,333$

$\ldots \qquad = \ldots$

6. $1 \times 8 + 1 = 9$

$12 \times 8 + 2 = 98$

$123 \times 8 + 3 = 987$

$\ldots \qquad = \ldots$

8. $1 + 2 + 1 \qquad = 2 \times 2$

$1 + 2 + 3 + 2 + 1 = 3 \times 3$

$1 + 2 + 3 + 4 + 3$

$\underline{\quad + 2 + 1} \qquad = 4 \times 4$

$\ldots \qquad = \ldots$

9.

						Sums of digits
		1				1
	1		1			2
	1	2	1			4
1		3	3	1		8
1	4	6	4	1		16
		. . . . . .				32

10. $1 + 2 + 3 = 6$

$4 + 5 + 6 = 6 + 9$

$7 + 8 + 9 = 6 + 9 + 9$

$10 + 11 + 12 = 6 + 9 + 9 + 9$

$\ldots \qquad = \ldots$

B. Magic squares

Study the numbers in this square.
Notice that the sum of the numbers in
each row, each column and each diagonal
adds to 15. The diagonal numbers are
those that run from corner to corner:

$(4, 5, 6)$ and $(2, 5, 8)$

4	9	2
3	5	7
8	1	6

A square such as this is called a *magic square*. The number 5
is always placed in the middle, and the numbers 1 to 9 are used
once only.

Here is another magic square using the numbers 1 to 9 once only.

4	3	8
9	5	1
2	7	6

Exercise 5 Copy each of the following and complete them to make magic squares. Numbers 1 to 9 must be used once only.

1.

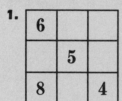

6		
	5	
8		4

3.

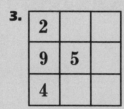

2		
9	5	
4		

5.

		3
6	1	8

2.

		8
	5	3
	9	

4.

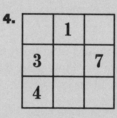

	1	
3		7
4		

6.

8	3	
1		9

Copy each of the following and complete them to make magic squares. Odd numbers 5 to 21 {5, 7, 9, 11, 13, 15, 17, 19, 21} must be used once only in each magic square. Each row, column and diagonal must add up to 39.

7.

	17	15
	13	
11		

9.

11		
21	13	
7		

8.

9	13	17
		7

10.

		7
5		21
	9	

Chapter Two

Notation and Numeration

Introduction

Notation and numeration deal with writing numbers in figures and words. They also deal with reading numbers which are written in figures.

A. Reading numbers

To write or read numbers in words it is helpful to place them under the following headings:

M, hT, tT, T, h, t, u

where

$$M = millions$$
$$hT = hundreds\ of\ thousands$$
$$tT = tens\ of\ thousands$$
$$T = thousands$$
$$h = hundreds$$
$$t = tens$$
$$u = units\ or\ ones$$

For example, read the following numbers: 420, 6075, 17 006, 250 010, 1 304 068.

Put the numbers under the above headings like this:

Thousands

M	hT	tT	T	h	t	u		
				4	2	0	=	Four hundred and twenty
			6	0	7	5	=	Six thousand and seventy-five
		1	7	0	0	6	=	Seventeen thousand and six
	2	5	0	0	1	0	=	Two hundred and fifty thousand and ten
1	3	0	4	0	6	8	=	One million three hundred and four thousand and sixty-eight

The numbers can now be read easily. Note that hT, tT and T represent the number of thousands.

Exercise 1 Read the following numbers:

1. 380		**6.** 3417		**11.** 16 000	
2. 702		**7.** 2074		**12.** 20 078	
3. 657		**8.** 4000		**13.** 36 012	
4. 89		**9.** 5010		**14.** 49 003	
5. 40		**10.** 1806		**15.** 40 001	
16. 200 000		**21.** 517 010		**26.** 3 000 000	
17. 243 708		**22.** 320 059		**27.** 5 600 000	
18. 315 610		**23.** 218 007		**28.** 2 140 010	
19. 143 229		**24.** 780 003		**29.** 7 014 753	
20. 640 741		**25.** 800 009		**30.** 8 006 732	
31. 3 610 073		**33.** 1 480 007		**35.** 4 000 007	
32. 6 006 143		**34.** 2 100 096			

B. Writing numbers in figures

To write twenty thousand and fifteen in figures we can use the same headings that were mentioned before:

Thousands

M	hT	tT	T	h	t	u
		2	0	0	1	5

We can ask: How many thousands? Answer 20, so 20 is written under the thousands heading. How many hundreds? Answer 0, so 0 is written under the hundreds heading. Then fifteen is 1 ten and 5 units. These are written under the tens and units headings respectively. Other numbers can be written similarly.

Examples   Write in figures:

	M	hT	tT	T	h	t	u
(a) Five thousand and eight =				5	0	0	8
(b) Twenty thousand and fifty =				2	0	0	5	0
(c) One hundred and five thousand and ten =		1	0	5	0	1	0
(d) Three million five hundred and eighteen thousand six hundred and fourteen =	3	5	1	8	6	1	4

Exercise 2   Write in figures:

1. Three hundred and eighty-seven.
2. Five hundred and seventy.
3. Nine hundred and eight.
4. Three thousand four hundred and eighteen.
5. Six thousand and forty.
6. Two thousand and six.
7. Eleven thousand three hundred and twenty-three.
8. Twenty-six thousand and forty-three.
9. Ten thousand and seventy.
10. Forty-nine thousand and three.
11. Thirty thousand and nine.
12. Three hundred thousand.
13. One hundred and fifty-three thousand six hundred and two.
14. Two hundred and ten thousand three hundred and twenty-one.
15. Four hundred and eleven thousand and twenty.

16. Eight hundred and twelve thousand and six.

17. Nine hundred thousand and nine.

18. One hundred and ten thousand and twenty-six.

19. Six hundred thousand and fourteen.

20. Three hundred and twelve thousand and ten.

21. Two million.

22. Three million four hundred thousand.

23. One million two hundred and forty thousand and thirty.

24. Five million and seven.

25. Two million five thousand and eighteen.

26. Five million and twenty-three.

27. Eight million one hundred and two.

28. Three million fourteen thousand eight hundred and four.

29. Six million three hundred and ten thousand and forty-two.

30. Two million three hundred thousand and eighty.

C. Expansion of numbers

The number 3746 can be expanded in the following way:
$$3746 = 3 \times 1000 + 7 \times 100 + 4 \times 10 + 6 \times 1$$

Similarly, the following numbers may be expanded in the same way:
$$2850 = 2 \times 1000 + 8 \times 100 + 5 \times 10$$
$$2207 = 2 \times 1000 + 2 \times 100 + 7 \times 1$$
$$486 = 4 \times 100 + 8 \times 10 + 6 \times 1$$
$$91 = 9 \times 10 + 1 \times 1$$

Exercise 3 Expand the following numbers like the examples above:

1. 87	**4.** 19	**7.** 223	**10.** 1643	**13.** 3005
2. 42	**5.** 70	**8.** 406	**11.** 2750	**14.** 4200
3. 28	**6.** 157	**9.** 380	**12.** 4030	**15.** 2107

Numbers can however be expanded differently:

Example

$$1823 = 18 \times 100 + 2 \times 10 + 3 \times 1$$
$$= 18 \times 100 + 23 \times 1$$
$$= 182 \times 10 + 3 \times 1$$
$$= 1 \times 1000 + 82 \times 10 + 3 \times 1$$
$$= 17 \times 100 + 12 \times 10 + 3 \times 1$$

Complete the following:

16. $815 = 8 \times 100 + \ldots \times 10 + 5 \times 1$

17. $75 = 7 \times \ldots + 5 \times 1$

18. $738 = \ldots \times 100 + 3 \times 10 + 8 \times 1$

19. $450 = \ldots \times 10$

20. $1356 = 1 \times \ldots + 35 \times 10 + 6 \times 1$

21. $197 = 1 \times 100 + \ldots \times 1$

22. $864 = 86 \times \ldots + 4 \times 1$

23. $2140 = \ldots \times 100 + 4 \times 10$

24. $876 = \ldots \times 10 + 6 \times 1$

25. $300 = \ldots \times 10$

26. $640 = \ldots$ tens

27. $387 = 3$ hundreds $+ 8$ tens $+ \ldots$ ones

28. $516 = \ldots$ hundreds $+ 21$ tens $+ 6$ ones

29. $827 = 8$ hundreds $+ \ldots$ ones

30. $1708 = 1$ thousand $+ \ldots$ tens $+ 8$ ones

31. $290 = 1$ hundred $+ \ldots$ tens

32. $5020 = \ldots$ tens

33. $76 = \ldots$ ones

34. $207 = \ldots$ tens $+ 7$ ones

35. $1004 = \ldots$ tens $+ 4$ ones

Examples

$$426 \times 43 = 426 \times 40 + 426 \times 3$$
$$207 \times 341 = 207 \times 300 + 207 \times 40 + 207 \times 1$$
$$83 \times 30 = 83 \times 3 \times 10$$

Complete the following:

36. $8 \times 40 = 8 \times 4 \times \ldots$

37. $4 \times 306 = 300 \times \ldots + 6 \times 4$

38. $89 \times 13 = 89 \times \ldots + 89 \times 3$

39. $53 \times 25 = 53 \times 20 + 53 \times \ldots$

40. $126 \times 40 = 126 \times 10 \times \ldots$

41. $94 \times 702 = 94 \times 700 + 94 \times \ldots$

42. $63 \times 241 = 63 \times \ldots + 63 \times 40 + 63 \times 1$

43. $627 \times 320 = 627 \times 300 + 627 \times \ldots$

44. $182 \times 60 = \ldots \times 6 \times 10$

45. $87 \times 390 = 87 \times 90 + 87 \times \ldots$

Write the answer for:

46. $300 + 70 + 6$

47. $500 + 20$

48. $1000 + 300 + 80 + 9$

49. $3000 + 90 + 7$

50. $6000 + 200 + 8$

51. $(2 \times 100) + (4 \times 10) + (3 \times 1)$

52. $(5 \times 1000) + (8 \times 100) + (6 \times 10) + (4 \times 1)$

53. $(4 \times 1000) + (5 \times 10) + (2 \times 1)$

54. $(2 \times 10\ 000) + (3 \times 100) + (5 \times 1)$

Chapter Three

Computation of Whole Numbers

A. Addition of whole numbers

Example $46 + 9 + 387 + 1076 = 1518$

$$
\begin{array}{r}
46 \\
9 \\
387 \\
+ 1076 \\
\hline
1518 \\
\end{array}
$$

_{2 2}

Exercise 1(a)

Add the following:

1.	34 + 23	**4.**	366 + 23	**7.**	87 + 56
2.	70 + 26	**5.**	435 12 + 151	**8.**	526 71 + 82
3.	94 + 65	**6.**	46 + 29	**9.**	605 9 + 73

10.	231	**12.**	508	**14.**	2175
	368		376		387
	+ 74		+ 482		1706
					+ 98

11.	126	**13.**	356	**15.**	63
	43		273		485
	60		281		6
	+ 475		+ 97		+ 1748

16. 31 + 48

17. 76 + 85

18. 23 + 4 + 61

19. 305 + 52 + 40

20. 732 + 43 + 82

21. 16 + 648 + 27

22. 56 + 589 + 23

23. 216 + 428 + 95

24. 1754 + 86 + 350 + 72

25. 372 + 2460 + 75 + 1243

26. 3470 + 81 + 2173 + 475

27. 2046 + 176 + 250

28. 1537 + 176 + 250

29. 84 + 23 + 1671

30. 164 + 3152 + 4076 + 237

Exercise 1(b)

1. Add together: two hundred and eight, seventy-six, and nine.

2. Add together: three thousand and ten, eighty-four, and nine hundred and eighty.

3. The difference between two numbers is 47. If one number is 38, what is the other number?

4. At our school there are 275 girls and 238 boys. How many pupils are at our school?

5. Mr Boyce the farmer has 19 cows, 47 pigs and 88 sheep. How many animals does he have?

6. Our school canteen sold 175 cakes on Monday, 168 on Wednesday and 154 on Friday. How many cakes were sold in the three days?

7. At our school there are 140 Infants, 172 Juniors and 88 Seniors. How many pupils are at our school?

8. One morning, a farmer picked 175 oranges, 358 mangoes, 1070 limes and 85 grapefruits. How many fruits did he pick in all?

9. On the first day of school, our teacher sold 185 mathematics workbooks, 216 English workbooks and 78 general knowledge workbooks. How many workbooks did she sell in all?

10. Find the sum of eighty-nine, one thousand and ten, and five hundred and sixty-seven.

11. A newspaper vendor sold 970 newspapers on Monday, 865 on Tuesday and 1089 on Wednesday. How many newspapers did he sell in the three days?

12. In the last four test matches a cricketer had scores of 64, 129, 85 and 7. How many did he score in the four matches?

B. Subtraction of whole numbers

Example $840 - 378 = 462$

$$\begin{array}{r} 840 \\ -378 \\ \hline 462 \end{array}$$

Exercise 2(a)

Subtract the following:

1. 84
    − 30

2. 93
    − 23

3. 76
    − 15

4. 486
    − 70

5. 926
    − 223

6. 830
    − 84

7. 743
    − 276

8. 1546
    − 472

9. 2530
    − 697

10.   5476
     − 1789
     _____

11. $84 - 50$ 19. $704 - 250$ 27. $3300 - 541$
12. $76 - 45$ 20. $643 - 134$ 28. $8215 - 3170$
13. $93 - 28$ 21. $1076 - 281$ 29. $6304 - 2783$
14. $378 - 36$ 22. $2148 - 753$ 30. $1763 - 88$
15. $748 - 213$ 23. $1372 - 482$ 31. $4870 - 390$
16. $643 - 129$ 24. $3106 - 278$ 32. $1135 - 746$
17. $826 - 571$ 25. $543 - 38$ 33. $4369 - 805$
18. $910 - 476$ 26. $1178 - 179$ 34. $6140 - 93$

Exercise 2(b)

1. From five thousand and one take three hundred and seven.

2. Take nine hundred and ten from six thousand and four.

3. What number must be added to 207 to make 300?

4. What number must I take from 104 to get 36?

5. The sum of two numbers is 180. If one number is 98, what is the other number?

6. What is the difference between 68 and 307?

7. Find the difference between 560 and 496.

8. A farmer had 300 chickens. He sold 164. How many had he left?

9. At our school there are 540 pupils. If there are 286 girls, how many boys are there?

10. At our school picnic there were 340 people. If there were 43 adults, how many children were there?

11. Mary had 200 cherries in a bag. If 36 of the cherries were bad, how many were good?

12. 3500 pupils wrote a certain examination. If 1726 of them failed, how many passed the examination?

C. Multiplication by one-digit numbers

Exercise 3(a)

Find:

1. 43 × 2	**15.** 606 × 5	**29.** 1678 × 4
2. 70 × 5	**16.** 307 × 9	**30.** 2070 × 6
3. 81 × 3	**17.** 812 × 8	**31.** 380 × 6
4. 62 × 4	**18.** 376 × 6	**32.** 803 × 3
5. 85 × 2	**19.** 540 × 7	**33.** 1769 × 4
6. 76 × 3	**20.** 284 × 5	**34.** 2915 × 2
7. 94 × 8	**21.** 600 × 9	**35.** 387 × 5
8. 68 × 6	**22.** 1208 × 6	**36.** 1540 × 7
9. 24 × 9	**23.** 743 × 8	**37.** 816 × 9
10. 67 × 7	**24.** 1324 × 7	**38.** 3040 × 3
11. 243 × 3	**25.** 786 × 9	**39.** 375 × 8
12. 183 × 4	**26.** 2079 × 4	**40.** 706 × 8
13. 704 × 2	**27.** 712 × 5	
14. 328 × 3	**28.** 384 × 7	

D. Multiplication by 10, 100, 1000 and multiples of these

Remember: To multiply a number by 10, just add one zero to the units side of that number. For example:

64 × 10 = 640;
one zero is added to 64

To multiply a number by 100, just add two zeros to the units side of that number. For example:

64 × 100 = 6400;
two zeros are added to 64

To multiply a number by 1000, just add three zeros to the units side of that figure. For example:

64 × 1000 = 64 000;
three zeros are added to 64

Exercise 3(b)

Find:

1.	8×10	**6.**	6×100	**11.**	5×1000
2.	27×10	**7.**	15×100	**12.**	11×1000
3.	40×10	**8.**	100×38	**13.**	43×1000
4.	315×10	**9.**	570×100	**14.**	1000×16
5.	10×37	**10.**	407×100	**15.**	50×1000

Examples Find   (a) 31×30 (b) 74×2000 (c) 400×86

Solutions

(a) $31 \times 30 = 31 \times 3 \times 10$
$$= 93 \times 10$$
$$= 930$$

$$\begin{array}{r} 31 \\ \times\ 3 \\ \hline 93 \end{array}$$

(b) $74 \times 2000 = 74 \times 2 \times 1000$
$$= 148 \times 1000$$
$$= 148\,000$$

$$\begin{array}{r} 74 \\ \times\ 2 \\ \hline 148 \end{array}$$

(c) $400 \times 86 = 86 \times 400$
$$= 86 \times 4 \times 100$$
$$= 344 \times 100$$
$$= 34\,400$$

$$\begin{array}{r} 86 \\ \times\ 4 \\ \hline 344 \\ {\scriptstyle 2} \end{array}$$

16.	41×20	**21.**	106×40	**26.**	18×70
17.	34×20	**22.**	80×50	**27.**	34×70
18.	22×30	**23.**	75×50	**28.**	80×88
19.	48×30	**24.**	61×60	**29.**	14×90
20.	29×40	**25.**	39×60	**30.**	380×90
31.	5×200	**36.**	18×500	**41.**	6×2000
32.	16×200	**37.**	600×23	**42.**	2000×7
33.	8×300	**38.**	57×700	**43.**	18×3000
34.	300×27	**39.**	31×800	**44.**	3000×16
35.	47×400	**40.**	900×26	**45.**	47×4000
46.	34×5000	**48.**	83×6000	**50.**	19×9000
47.	5000×71	**49.**	7×7000		

E. Multiplication by two-and three-digit numbers

Examples   Find   **(a)** 63×34 **(b)** 176×307 **(c)** 248×356
(d) 37×580

Solutions   **(a)** $63 \times 34 = 63 \times 30 + 63 \times 4$
$= 1890 + 252$
$= 2142$

$$
\begin{array}{r}
63 \\
\times\ 34 \\
\hline
1890 \quad (63 \times 30) \\
+\quad 252 \quad (63 \times 4) \\
\hline
2142 \quad (63 \times 34) \\
\end{array}
$$

(b) $176 \times 307 = 176 \times 300 + 176 \times 7$
$= 52\,800 + 1232$
$= 54\,032$

$$
\begin{array}{r}
176 \\
\times\ 307 \\
\hline
52\,800 \quad (176 \times 300) \\
+\quad 1\,232 \quad (176 \times 7) \\
\hline
54\,032 \quad (176 \times 307) \\
\end{array}
$$

(c) $248 \times 256 = 248 \times 200 + 248 \times 50$
$+\ 248 \times 6$
$= 49\,600 + 12\,400$
$+\ 1488$
$= 63\,488$

$$
\begin{array}{r}
248 \\
\times\ 256 \\
\hline
49\,600 \quad (248 \times 200) \\
12\,400 \quad (248 \times 50) \\
+\quad 1\,488 \quad (248 \times 6) \\
\hline
63\,488 \quad (248 \times 256) \\
\end{array}
$$

(d) $37 \times 580 = 37 \times 500 + 37 \times 80$
$= 18\,500 + 2960$
$= 21\,460$

$$
\begin{array}{r}
37 \\
\times\ 580 \\
\hline
18\,500 \quad (37 \times 500) \\
+\quad 2\,960 \quad (37 \times 80) \\
\hline
21\,460 \quad (37 \times 580) \\
\end{array}
$$

Exercise 3(c)

Find:

1. 73×14	**4.** 83×18	**7.** 23×32
2. 46×13	**5.** 42×17	**8.** 83×23
3. 78×12	**6.** 62×22	**9.** 76×24

10. 33×42,	**21.** 39×410	**32.** 315×624
11. 143×36	**22.** 227×320	**33.** 79×127
12. 204×27	**23.** 270×380	**34.** 803×246
13. 351×62	**24.** 276×110	**35.** 927×276
14. 487×71	**25.** 274×304	**36.** 147×211
15. 132×34	**26.** 206×804	**37.** 230×336
16. 280×43	**27.** 180×705	**38.** 407×413
17. 460×31	**28.** 120×764	**39.** 370×116
18. 703×42	**29.** 340×267	**40.** 223×620
19. 196×73	**30.** 517×168	
20. 288×26	**31.** 270×347	

Exercise 3(d)

1. Find the product of 67 and 40.
2. What number divided by 6 gives 12?
3. What number must be divided by 5 to get 20?
4. Multiply eight hundred and seven by eleven.
5. A case contains 24 soft drinks. How many soft drinks would 8 similar cases contain?
6. What is the answer when twenty-five is multiplied by itself?
7. A box contains 40 packs of chocolates. If each pack contains 10 chocolates, how many chocolates are in the box?
8. At our school party there were 45 tables. If 6 pupils sit at each table, how many pupils were sitting at the 45 tables?
9. A minimart has 6 shelves for corned beef. If there are 470 tins of corned beef on each shelf, how many tins of corned beef are on the 6 shelves?
10. Mr Walkes the village farmer sells 55 L of milk every day. How many litres of milk would he sell in 7 days?
11. A minibus carries 35 passengers on every trip. How many passengers had it carried after 16 trips?
12. A teacher divided a box of biscuits equally among 25 pupils. If each pupil got 12 biscuits, how many biscuits were in the box?

F. Division by one-digit numbers

Examples   Find (a) $581 \div 7$

(b) $648 \div 6$

(c) $313 \div 9$

Solutions   (a) $581 \div 7 = 83$ $7\overline{)581}$
                                              083

(b) $648 \div 6 = 108$ $6\overline{)648}$
                                              108

(c) $313 \div 9 = 34 \,\text{R}\, 7$ $9\overline{)313}$
                                              $034 \,\text{R}\, 7$

Note that in **(c)** there is a remainder of 7.

Exercise 4(a)

Find the following, remembering to give the remainder where necessary:

1. $46 \div 2$	**15.** $486 \div 9$	**29.** $8120 \div 9$
2. $184 \div 2$	**16.** $440 \div 8$	**30.** $7640 \div 6$
3. $90 \div 2$	**17.** $372 \div 6$	**31.** $4619 \div 4$
4. $60 \div 3$	**18.** $581 \div 7$	**32.** $1400 \div 8$
5. $84 \div 4$	**19.** $224 \div 9$	**33.** $2170 \div 6$
6. $90 \div 5$	**20.** $271 \div 5$	**34.** $3743 \div 5$
7. $186 \div 6$	**21.** $729 \div 9$	**35.** $2448 \div 6$
8. $204 \div 4$	**22.** $463 \div 5$	**36.** $1632 \div 8$
9. $175 \div 2$	**23.** $630 \div 7$	**37.** $1170 \div 5$
10. $309 \div 5$	**24.** $500 \div 6$	**38.** $9252 \div 3$
11. $252 \div 6$	**25.** $403 \div 8$	**39.** $7301 \div 7$
12. $725 \div 5$	**26.** $4730 \div 5$	**40.** $4560 \div 4$
13. $832 \div 8$	**27.** $3175 \div 3$	
14. $729 \div 7$	**28.** $3241 \div 7$	

G. Long division

The following rule will help us in doing long division:

Rule for long division

(1) Match and try a number.

(2) Multiply the number tried by the divisor.

(3) Subtract.

(4) Take down the next figure.

Examples Find **(a)** $441 \div 21$ **(b)** $1807 \div 17$

Solutions **(a)** $441 \div 21 = 21$

$$
\begin{array}{r}
021 \\
21\overline{\smash)441} \\
-\,42 \\
\hline
21 \\
-\,21 \\
\hline
00
\end{array}
$$

Step 1. 21 into 4 cannot go so put a zero
21 into 44, try 2

Step 2. Multiply: $21 \times 2 = 42$

Step 3. Subtract: $44 - 42 = 2$

Step 4. Take down the next figure, which is 1

Step 1. 21 into 21, try 1

Step 2. Multiply: $21 \times 1 = 21$

Step 3. Subtract: $21 - 21 = 0$

(b) $1807 \div 17 = 106\,\text{R}\,5$

$$
\begin{array}{r}
106 \\
17\overline{\smash)1807} \\
-\,17 \\
\hline
107 \\
-\,107 \\
\hline
005
\end{array}
$$

Step 1. 17 into 1 cannot go so put a zero
17 into 18, try 1

Step 2. Multiply: $17 \times 1 = 17$

Step 3. Subtract: $18 - 17 = 1$

Step 4. Take down the next figure, which is 0

Step 1. 17 into 10 cannot go so put a zero

Steps 2. and *3.* can be omitted here

Step 4. Take down the next figure, which is 7

Step 1. 17 into 107, try 6

Step 2. Multiply: $17 \times 6 = 102$

Step 3. Subtract: $107 - 102 = 5$
5 is the remainder

Exercise 4(b)

Find the following, remembering to give the remainder where necessary:

1. $231 \div 21$	**21.** $250 \div 25$	**41.** $3980 \div 18$
2. $651 \div 21$	**22.** $425 \div 25$	**42.** $3546 \div 29$
3. $861 \div 21$	**23.** $375 \div 25$	**43.** $4312 \div 14$
4. $1071 \div 21$	**24.** $1625 \div 25$	**44.** $3076 \div 27$
5. $1281 \div 21$	**25.** $1875 \div 25$	**45.** $6090 \div 29$
6. $341 \div 31$	**26.** $294 \div 14$	**46.** $8176 \div 28$
7. $651 \div 31$	**27.** $357 \div 17$	**47.** $3983 \div 71$
8. $961 \div 31$	**28.** $378 \div 18$	**48.** $8576 \div 63$
9. $1261 \div 31$	**29.** $589 \div 19$	**49.** $1326 \div 46$
10. $1581 \div 31$	**30.** $496 \div 16$	**50.** $946 \div 43$
11. $451 \div 41$	**31.** $4860 \div 12$	**51.** $7321 \div 32$
12. $861 \div 41$	**32.** $864 \div 27$	**52.** $3700 \div 19$
13. $1312 \div 41$	**33.** $672 \div 32$	**53.** $8410 \div 25$
14. $8405 \div 41$	**34.** $5304 \div 26$	**54.** $6800 \div 34$
15. $1681 \div 41$	**35.** $7585 \div 37$	**55.** $4860 \div 12$
16. $2460 \div 20$	**36.** $7321 \div 32$	**56.** $4560 \div 15$
17. $2640 \div 20$	**37.** $3700 \div 19$	**57.** $4617 \div 23$
18. $8460 \div 20$	**38.** $1505 \div 35$	**58.** $814 \div 37$
19. $6390 \div 30$	**39.** $4446 \div 38$	**59.** $1275 \div 15$
20. $4800 \div 40$	**40.** $5400 \div 15$	**60.** $4310 \div 25$

Exercise 4(c)

1. Divide three hundred and four by eight.
2. By what number must I multiply 12 to get 192?
3. Divide 280 plums equally among 5 girls. How many plums does each girl get?
4. A fisherman caught 2000 flying fish. He sold the same number of flying fish to each of 8 buyers. How many flying fish did each buyer receive?
5. How many times can 11 be taken from 176?

6. A crate can hold 30 eggs. How many crates are required to hold 210 eggs?

7. What is the remainder when 3140 is divided by 12?

8. 270 marbles are arranged in 6 rows. If each row contains the same number of marbles, how many marbles are in each row?

9. Our form captain divided 104 markers equally among 8 groups of children. How many markers did each group receive?

10. Esther's Variety sold 740 turnovers to children from our school. If each child bought 5 turnovers, how many children from our school bought turnovers?

11. On one side of our village there are 36 houses. If every other house is painted yellow, how many houses are painted yellow?

12. Our class collected the same number of stamps each day for 11 days. If the class collected 165 stamps, how many stamps were collected each day?

H. Using multiplication and division facts

We can use the multiplication and division facts to give answers to some problems involving multiplication and division.

For example $10 \times 12 = 120$

From this we can find answers for:

(a) 10×24 (b) 10×6

(a) $10 \times 24 = 120 \times 2$
$= 240$
(Comparing this question with the example above, note that 10 remains the same while 12 is now doubled. Therefore to get the answer we must multiply 120 by 2)

(b) $10 \times 6 = 120 \div 2$
$= 60$
(Comparing this question with the example above, note that 10 remains the same while 12 is now halved. Therefore to get the answer we must divide 120 by 2)

Examples (1)
$$10 \times 12 = 120$$
$$120 \div 10 = 12$$
$$120 \div 12 = 10$$

Find   **(a)** $120 \div 20$ **(b)** $120 \div 6$

(a) $120 \div 20 = 12 \div 2$
$\qquad\qquad\qquad = 6$

(Comparing **(a)** with the example above, 120 remains the same while 10 is now doubled. Therefore to get the answer, 12 must be halved)

(b) $120 \div 6 = 10 \times 2$
$\qquad\qquad\quad = 20$

(Comparing **(b)** with the example above, 120 remains the same while 12 is now halved. Therefore to get the answer, 10 must be doubled)

Examples (2) Look at the worked problem below and then use it to give answers to the questions alongside.

$$
\begin{array}{r}
14 \\
\times\, 24 \\
\hline
280 \\
56 \\
\hline
336 \\
\hline
\end{array}
$$

Find   **(a)** $14 \times 24 - 14 \times 20$

(b) $14 \times 24 - 14 \times 4$

(c) 14×25

(a) $14 \times 24 - 14 \times 20 = 336 - 280$
$\qquad\qquad\qquad\qquad\qquad = 56$

(b) $14 \times 24 - 14 \times 4 = 336 - 56$
$\qquad\qquad\qquad\qquad\qquad = 280$

(c) $14 \times 25 = 14 \times 24 + 14 \times 1$
$\qquad\qquad\quad = 336 + 14$
$\qquad\qquad\quad = 350$

Exercise 5   Look at the worked problem to the right and then answer the following questions.

1. 16×10 **2.** 16×8

3. $16 \times 18 - 16 \times 8$

4. $16 \times 18 - 16 \times 10$

5. 16×19

6. 16×17 **7.** 16×20

$$
\begin{array}{r}
16 \\
\times\, 18 \\
\hline
160 \\
+\, 128 \\
\hline
288 \\
\hline
\end{array}
$$

Given that $32 \times 22 = 704$, find:

8. 22×32 **10.** 32×44 **12.** 8×22

9. 32×11 **11.** 64×11 **13.** 64×44

Given that $704 \div 44 = 16$, find:

14. $704 \div 16$ **17.** $1408 \div 22$ **20.** $352 \div 11$

15. $704 \div 11$ **18.** $1408 \div 44$

16. $704 \div 44$ **19.** $352 \div 22$

I. Order of operation

You will be are quite familiar with the four arithmetic operations of addition, subtraction, multiplication and division. However, when two or three operations appear together in a problem, you need to know which operations are to be done first, second and third. The following examples will illustrate the order of performing operations.

Examples   Find the value of   **(a)** $\quad 9 - 4 + 1$
                              (b) $\quad 24 \div 4 - 2$
                              (c) $\quad 8 + 3 \times 6 - 5$
                              (d) $\quad (2 + 5) \times (7 - 4)$

Solutions   **(a)** $\quad 9 - 4 + 1$ first subtract
                 $= 5 + 1$ then add
                 $= 6$
       or $9 - 4 + 1$
                 $= 9 + 1 - 4$ first add
                 $= 10 - 4$ then subtract
                 $= 6$

Note: You may either add first and then subtract, or subtract first and then add.

     (b) $\quad 24 \div 4 - 2$ first divide
                 $= 6 - 2$ then subtract
                 $= 4$

(c) $8 + 3 \times 6 - 5$ first multiply
$= 8 + 18 - 5$ then add
$= 26 - 5$ then subtract
$= 21$

Note: Multiplication and division are done *before* addition and subtraction.

(d) $(2 + 5) \times (7 - 4)$ first do brackets
$= 7 \times 3$ then multiply
$= 21$

Note: If a problem involves brackets, these must be done *first*.

So the order is: the brackets must be done first; then multiplication and division are done next; and addition and subtraction are done last.

Exercise 6   Find the value of:

1. $7 - 5 + 4$

2. $6 + 8 - 10$

3. $15 - 4 + 3$

4. $12 - 5 - 4$

5. $5 \times 4 + 3$

6. $6 + 8 \div 2$

7. $10 - 2 \times 3$

8. $8 \div 4 - 2$

9. $6 \times 3 + 2 \times 7$

10. $4 \times 8 - 6 \times 2$

11. $12 \div 4 + 10 \div 5$

12. $(3 + 4) \times 3$

13. $8 \times (5 + 2)$

14. $(6 - 4) \times 10$

15. $(5 + 7) \div 4$

16. $(4 + 6) \div (3 + 2)$

17. $15 \div (6 - 1)$

18. $(8 - 2) \times (8 - 1)$

19. $(5 + 0) \times (9 - 0)$

20. $8 \times (4 + 1) - 3$

21. $6 + 3 \times 4 - 1$

22. $18 - 2 \times 7 + 6$

23. $3 \times 2 + 4 \times 6 - 5$

24. $(8 - 3) \div (3 + 2)$

25. $8 + 6 \times 3$

26. $10 + 4 \div 2$

27. $9 \div 3 + 6$

28. $(4 + 1) \times (5 - 3) - 6$

29. $12 \times (8 - 5)$

30. $6 + 4 - 1$

31. $8 \times 3 + 2 - 4$

32. $6 + 6 \div 2 + 1$

33. $(4 + 2) \times 3 + 6$

34. $4 \times 0 + 7$

35. $(3 \times 3) - (2 \times 2)$	**38.** $10 - (8 - 2) \div 3$
36. $12 \div (2 \times 3)$	**39.** $9 + (7 - 3) \times 4$
37. $2 \times (6 - 4) \times (3 + 7)$	**40.** $8 \times (6 - 6)$

J. Problems involving more than one operation

Some problems require more than one operation for their solution. For instance, a problem may require addition and subtraction to solve it.

Example (1) A fruit vendor bought 200 fruits. She bought 35 grapefruits, 70 oranges and some mangoes. How many mangoes did she buy?

Solution Number of grapefruits + oranges bought $= 35 + 70 = 105$

∴ Number of mangoes $= 200 - 105 = 95$

The following problem requires two operations for its solution. Both operations are multiplication.

Example (2) A carton contains 20 cases of red stripe malts. If each case contains 24 malts, how many malts would 5 similar cartons contain?

Solution 1 carton contains 20 cases

∴ 5 cartons contain $20 \times 5 = 100$ cases

1 case contains 24 malts

∴ 100 cases contain $24 \times 100 = 2400$ malts

Exercise 7
1. What is three times twelve plus eighteen?
2. Six times a certain number plus three equals 51. What is the number?
3. What number when divided by 12 gives 14 remainder 5?
4. Mary picked 240 cherries. She gave 68 to Jane and 75 to Harriet. How many had she left?

5. Our teacher had a box containing 140 markers. There were 28 blue markers, 17 red markers, 35 green markers and the other markers were yellow. How many markers were yellow?

6. A book contains 110 pages. Pages 17 to 26 contain pictures. How many pages do not contain pictures?

7. A bus started its journey with 65 passengers. During the journey 25 passengers got off and 17 got on. How many passengers were in the bus at the end of the journey?

8. A box contains 4 rows of eggs with 12 eggs in each row. If these eggs are arranged in 6 rows, how many eggs would be in each row?

9. Six times 12 is equal to four times a number. What is the number?

10. What must be added to the product of 7 and 8 to make 60?

11. What must be subtracted from the sum of 46 and 58 to leave 76?

12. What is the smallest number that must be subtracted from 80 to make a number that can be divided exactly by 12?

13. What number must be added to the sum of 25 and 48 to make 120?

14. What is the smallest number that must be added to 107 to make a number that is exactly divisible by 7.

15. Add the sum of 8 and 24 to the product of 3 and 24.

16. Add the difference of 27 and 9 to the difference of 36 and 9.

17. From the sum of 40 and 20 take twice 18.

18. On Friday, a fisherman caught 35 dolphins. On Saturday, he caught thrice as many dolphins as he caught on Friday. How many dolphins altogether did he catch for the two days?

19. An express minibus carries 35 passengers on every trip. If the minibus makes 10 trips a day, how many passengers in all will the minibus carry for 5 days?

20. Mr Broomes had a certain number of pencils. He gave 16 boys 9 pencils each and had 6 pencils left over. How many pencils did Mr Broomes have?

Chapter Four

Using the Signs
$+, -, \times, \div,$
$<, =, >$

Examples For each question use two signs from here $(+, -, \times, \div)$, one in each space, to make each statement correct:

(a) $6 \ldots 4 = 12 \ldots 2$ **(b)** $7 \ldots 2 = 8 \ldots 6$

(c) $5 \ldots 4 = 8 \ldots 8$ **(d)** $4 \ldots 3 \ldots 5 = 7$

(e) $(6 \ldots 2) \ldots 3 = 12$

Solutions **(a)** $6 + 4 = 12 - 2$ **(b)** $7 \times 2 = 8 + 6$

(c) $5 - 4 = 8 \div 8$ **(d)** $4 \times 3 - 5 = 7$

(e) $(6 - 2) \times 3 = 12$

Exercise 1 For each question use two signs from here $(+, -, \times, \div)$, one in each space, to make each statement correct:

1. $9 \ldots 2 = 3 \ldots 4$	**8.** $42 \ldots 6 = 15 \ldots 8$
2. $8 \ldots 1 = 5 \ldots 3$	**9.** $12 \ldots 2 = 10 \ldots 1$
3. $3 \ldots 4 = 15 \ldots 3$	**10.** $64 \ldots 8 = 56 \ldots 7$
4. $24 \ldots 12 = 2 \ldots 0$	**11.** $27 \ldots 3 = 9 \ldots 0$
5. $7 \ldots 4 = 15 \ldots 13$	**12.** $5 \ldots 5 = 8 \ldots 2$
6. $9 \ldots 9 = 7 \ldots 0$	**13.** $16 \ldots 8 = 6 \ldots 3$
7. $6 \ldots 0 = 15 \ldots 9$	**14.** $3 \ldots 4 = 12 \ldots 1$

15.	$4 \ldots 5 = 24 \ldots 4$	**18.**	$6 \ldots 3 = 9 \ldots 1$
16.	$2 \ldots 4 = 40 \ldots 5$	**19.**	$8 \ldots 7 = 14 \ldots 4$
17.	$24 \ldots 4 = 18 \ldots 12$	**20.**	$15 \ldots 15 = 2 \ldots 2$

21.	$5 \ldots 4 \ldots 3 = 12$	**31.**	$10 \ldots (3 \ldots 2) = 4$
22.	$7 \ldots 0 \ldots 4 = 4$	**32.**	$6 \ldots 4 \ldots 3 = 7$
23.	$(13 \ldots 8) \ldots 2 = 10$	**33.**	$(7 \ldots 2) \ldots 2 = 18$
24.	$(4 \ldots 2) \ldots 3 = 18$	**34.**	$2 \ldots 2 \ldots 2 = 8$
25.	$12 \ldots (4 \ldots 2) = 2$	**35.**	$15 \ldots 8 \ldots 3 = 10$
26.	$9 \ldots 5 \ldots 1 = 15$	**36.**	$(8 \ldots 2) \ldots 5 = 2$
27.	$16 \ldots 8 \ldots 4 = 6$	**37.**	$14 \ldots 7 \ldots 3 = 5$
28.	$10 \ldots 3 \ldots 3 = 4$	**38.**	$6 \ldots 4 \ldots 10 = 14$
29.	$1 \ldots 1 \ldots 1 = 0$	**39.**	$12 \ldots 5 \ldots 5 = 2$
30.	$12 \ldots (2 \ldots 4) = 4$	**40.**	$5 \ldots 0 \ldots 3 = 3$

In this next section remember that $<$ means less than
$=$ means equal to
$>$ means greater than

Examples Put a sign from here ($<$, $=$, $>$) in each space to make each statement true:

(a) $4 + 1 \ldots 8 \times 0$ (b) $6 \times 6 \ldots 4 \times 9$

(c) $9 - 2 \ldots 5 + 7$

Solutions (a) $4 + 1 = 5$ (b) $6 \times 6 = 36$
$8 \times 0 = 0$ $4 \times 9 = 36$
$\therefore$ 5 is greater than 0 $\therefore$ 36 is equal to 36
$\therefore$ $4 + 1 > 8 \times 0$ $\therefore$ $6 \times 6 = 4 \times 9$

(c) $9 - 2 = 7$
$5 + 7 = 12$
$\therefore$ 7 is less than 12
$\therefore$ $9 - 2 < 5 + 7$

Exercise 2 Put a sign from here (<, =, >) in each space to make each statement true:

1. 5 ... 8
2. 12 ... 3
3. 2 + 4 ... 8
4. 10 − 3 ... 6
5. 5 ... 2 + 8
6. 6 ... 3 × 2
7. 2 × 5 ... 9 + 2
8. 14 − 3 ... 3 × 4
9. 27 − 9 ... 36 − 12
10. 5 × 5 ... 8 + 2

11. 9 × 0 ... 3 + 4
12. 20 − 5 ... 4 × 1
13. 3 × 3 ... 3 + 3
14. 10 − 0 ... 10 × 1
15. 40 − 8 ... 9 − 7
16. 100 − 16 ... 8 × 12
17. 4 × 12 ... 11 × 5
18. 56 − 7 ... 54 − 6
19. 7 × 0 ... 12 × 0
20. 14 − 0 ... 11 − 11

21. 4 × 7 ... 5 × 6
22. 32 − 7 ... 16 + 9
23. 1 × 1 ... 1 + 1
24. 48 − 6 ... 15 − 3
25. 70 − 14 ... 6 × 9

26. 12 × 0 ... 8 × 0
27. 15 × 1 ... 15 − 1
28. 84 − 12 ... 3 × 7
29. 6 × 7 ... 36 + 8
30. 13 + 0 ... 13 − 0

Chapter Five

Factors and Multiples

A. Factors

$$12 = 3 \times 4$$
$$= 2 \times 6$$
$$= 1 \times 12$$

1, 2, 3, 4, 6 and 12 can divide into 12 exactly.

These numbers are called the factors of 12.

The *factors* of a number are those numbers which can divide it *exactly*.

Examples   Find the factors of   **(a)** 10   **(b)** 18

Solutions   **(a)**   Factors of 10 = (1, 2, 5, 10)

(b)   Factors of 18 = (1, 2, 3, 6, 9, 18)

Note that 1 is a factor of *any* number. And the number itself is a factor of itself. For example, 10 is a factor of 10, and 18 is a factor of 18.

Exercise 1   List all the factors of:

1. 4	**4.** 9	**7.** 16	**10.** 22	**13.** 28
2. 5	**5.** 14	**8.** 20	**11.** 24	**14.** 30
3. 8	**6.** 15	**9.** 21	**12.** 26	**15.** 32

Which of the numbers (2, 3, 5, 7, 9, 15) are factors of:

16. 35   **17.** 45   **18.** 63

Which of the numbers (1, 2, 3, 4, 6, 9, 12, 16) are factors of:

19. 36   **20.** 54   **21.** 64

22. Which of the numbers (1, 2, 4, 5, 6, 8, 10, 12, 15, 20, 40) are not factors of 40?

B. Prime factors

We have learnt already that the factors of 12 are 1, 2, 3, 4, 6 and 12. Of these, only 2 and 3 are prime numbers. Thus 2 and 3 are called the *prime factors* of 12.

Example What are the prime factors of 15?

Solution Factors of 15 $=$ (1, 3, 5, 15)
Prime factors of 15 $=$ (3, 5)

Exercise 2 What are the prime factors of:

1. 10   **6.** 30

2. 14   **7.** 35

3. 21   **8.** 51

4. 26   **9.** 95

5. 28   **10.** 105

C. Expressing a number as a product of prime factors

Example (1) Express 60 as a product of prime factors.

Solution $60 = 2 \times 2 \times 3 \times 5$

$$\begin{array}{r|r} 2 & 60 \\ \hline 2 & 30 \\ \hline 3 & 15 \\ \hline 5 & 05 \\ \hline & 1 \end{array}$$

Note that only prime numbers* are chosen to do the continuous division. The division is done until the answer is exactly 1.

*See p. 40.

Example (2)   Express 100 as a product of prime factors.

Solution $100 = 2 \times 2 \times 5 \times 5$

$$\begin{array}{r|r} 2 & 100 \\ 2 & 50 \\ 5 & 25 \\ 5 & 05 \\ \hline & 1 \end{array}$$

Exercise 3   Express the following numbers as a product of prime factors:

1.	4	**6.**	20	**11.**	45	**16.**	64
2.	8	**7.**	22	**12.**	50	**17.**	140
3.	12	**8.**	24	**13.**	75	**18.**	200
4.	16	**9.**	33	**14.**	81	**19.**	210
5.	18	**10.**	42	**15.**	102	**20.**	324

D. Multiples

The multiples of a number are found by multiplying *that number* by 1, 2, 3, 4, 5, 6 . . . (the 3 dots mean 'and so on').

Examples   (1)   The multiples of 3 are (3, 6, 9, 12, 15, 18 . . .).

(2)   The multiples of 4 that are less than 25 are (4, 8, 12, 16, 20, 24).

(3)   The multiples of 8 between 0 and 50 are (8, 16, 24, 32, 40, 48).

Exercise 4   List:

1.   The multiples of 2 that are less than 11.

2.   The multiples of 5 that are less than 30.

3.   The multiples of 6 between 0 and 40.

4.   The multiples of 7 between 1 and 50.

5.   The first 5 multiples of 10.

6.   Which of the numbers (2, 4, 6, 12, 16) are not multiples of 4?

List the next two multiples in each sequence:

7.	21,	24,	27,	. . .,	. . .
8.	12,	36,	48,	. . .,	. . .
9.	9,	18,	27,	. . .,	. . .
10.	10,	15,	20,	. . .,	. . .

E. Lowest common multiple (L.C.M.)

Example (1) Find the L.C.M. of 2 and 3.

Solution Multiples of 2 = (2, 4, 6, 8, 10, 12 . . .)
Multiples of 3 = (3, 6, 9, 12, 15, 18 . . .)
Common multiples of 2 and 3 = (6, 12 . . .)
L.C.M. of 2 and 3 = 6

Note that we list a number of multiples of the numbers involved until a common multiple appears.

Example (2) Find the L.C.M. of 3, 4 and 6.

Solution Multiples of 3 = (3, 6, 9, ⑫, 15, 18 . . .)

Multiples of 4 = (4, 8, ⑫, 16, 20, 24 . . .)

Multiples of 6 = (6, ⑫, 18, 24, 30, 36 . . .)

L.C.M. of 3, 4 and 6 = 12

Exercise 5 Find the L.C.M. of:

1.	2 and 6	6.	6 and 8
2.	2 and 4	7.	2, 3 and 4
3.	2 and 5	8.	2, 3 and 5
4.	3 and 4	9.	6 and 10
5.	3 and 8		

Study this diagram, that shows numbers up to and including 30, and then answer question 10.

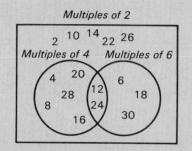

10. What is the L.C.M. of 2, 4 and 6?

Chapter Six

Some Sets of Numbers

A. Whole numbers

Whole numbers are consecutive numbers; that is, numbers that follow one another. The first whole number is zero (0).

For instance, the first 5 whole numbers are (0, 1, 2, 3, 4), and the whole numbers between 11 and 15 are (12, 13, 14).

Example   The sum of 3 consecutive whole numbers is 27. Find them.

Solution   The middle number is $\dfrac{27}{3} = 9$

So the three numbers are 8, 9 and 10.

B. Natural numbers

Natural numbers are also consecutive numbers. The first natural number is one (1).

For instance, the first 5 natural numbers are (1, 2, 3, 4, 5), and the natural numbers greater than 6 but less than 12 are (7, 8, 9, 10, 11).

Example   The sum of 5 consecutive natural numbers is 65. Find them.

Solution   The middle number is $\dfrac{65}{5} = 13$

So the 5 numbers are 11, 12, 13, 14 and 15.

Exercise 1   List:

   1. The first 4 whole numbers.

   2. The first 6 natural numbers.

   3. The set of whole numbers between 10 and 17.

   4. The set of natural numbers between 10 and 17.

   5. The set of natural numbers greater than 25 but less than 30.

   6. The set of whole numbers less than 6.

   7. The sum of 3 consecutive whole numbers is 30. What are the 3 numbers?

   8. The sum of 5 consecutive natural numbers is 60. Find the 5 numbers.

C. Even numbers

An *even number* is one that can be divided exactly by 2. Here are the first 5 even numbers:

(0, 2, 4, 6, 8)

Question: Is 96 an even number? $2\rfloor\overline{96}$

96 can be divided by 2 exactly $\overline{48}$

Answer: 96 is an even number.

Remember that all even numbers must *end* in one of the following even numbers (0, 2, 4, 6, 8).

Exercise 2   Write the next two even numbers in each sequence:

1.	4,	6,	8,	. . . , . . .
2.	16,	18,	20,	. . . , . . .
3.	30,	32,	34,	. . . , . . .
4.	52,	54,	56,	. . . , . . .
5.	68,	70,	72,	. . . , . . .
6.	76,	78,	80,	. . . , . . .
7.	100,	102,	104,	. . . , . . .
8.	152,	154,	156,	. . . , . . .
9.	224,	226,	228,	. . . , . . .
10.	318,	320,	322,	. . . , . . .

11. Pick out all the even numbers from the list:
(7, 14, 19, 27, 31, 40, 48, 57, 63, 72, 93, 120, 215, 270)

Use all of the digits (4, 1, 6) *once only* to write

12. the largest possible even number

13. the smallest possible even number.

Use all of the digits (2, 3, 5, 8) *once only* to write

14. the largest possible even number

15. the smallest possible even number.

List

16. all the even numbers between 10 and 20

17. all the even numbers between 31 and 41

18. all the even numbers less than 15.

19. The sum of 3 consecutive even numbers is 66. What are the three numbers?

20. The sum of 5 consecutive even numbers is 100. What are the 5 numbers?

D. Odd numbers

An *odd number* is a number which, when divided by 2, gives the remainder 1. Here are the first 5 odd numbers:

(1, 3, 5, 7, 9)

Question: Is 47 an odd number?

47 when divided by 2 gives the remainder 1

Answer: 47 is an odd number.

$$2 \overline{\smash{\big)}\, 47}$$
$$23\ \text{R}\ 1$$

Remember that all odd numbers must *end* in one of the following odd numbers (1, 3, 5, 7, 9).

Exercise 3 Write the next two odd numbers in each sequence:

1.	7,	9,	11,	...,	...
2.	19,	21,	23,	...,	...
3.	33,	35,	37,	...,	...
4.	57,	59,	61,	...,	...
5.	71,	73,	75,	...,	...
6.	93,	95,	97,	...,	...
7.	111,	113,	115,	...,	...
8.	135,	137,	139,	...,	...
9.	159,	161,	163,	...,	...
10.	207,	209,	211,	...,	...

11. Pick out all the odd numbers from the list:
(12, 17, 31, 43, 46, 47, 70, 74, 91, 105, 108, 110, 121, 168)

Use all the digits (5, 3, 8) *once only* to write

12. the largest possible odd number

13. the smallest possible odd number.

Use all of the digits (1, 7, 6, 2) *once only* to write

14. the largest possible odd number

15. the smallest possible odd number.

List

16. all the odd numbers less than 16

17. all the odd numbers between 10 and 20

18. all the odd numbers between 30 and 40.

19. The sum of 3 consecutive odd numbers is 75. What are the 3 numbers?

20. The sum of 5 consecutive odd numbers is 85. What are the 5 numbers?

E. Prime numbers

A *prime number* is a number that has only *two* distinct factors, *itself* and *one*. So 1 is not a prime number.

Example   Which of the following are prime numbers?

2, 9, 13, 15

Solution   Factors of 2 are (1, 2)

Factors of 9 are (1, 3, 9)

Factors of 13 are (1, 13)

Factors of 15 are (1, 3, 5, 15)

2 and 13 are prime numbers because they have only *two* factors. 9 and 15 have more than two factors and are not prime numbers. Remember that 2 is the only even prime number. All the other prime numbers are odd; but not all odd numbers are prime numbers.

Exercise 4 List:

1. The first 5 prime numbers.

2. The prime numbers between 10 and 20.

3. The prime numbers which are greater than 20 but less than 30.

4. The set of even prime numbers.

5. The prime numbers which are factors of 26.

Write the next two prime numbers in each sequence:

6.	2,	3,	5,	7, . . . , . . .
7.	17,	19,	23,	. . . , . . .
8.	37,	41,	43,	. . . , . . .
9.	53,	59,	61,	. . . , . . .

10. Which of the numbers (3, 6, 11, 15, 17, 21, 25, 27, 29, 31, 33, 39) are prime numbers?

Exercise 5   1. Which of these are not prime numbers: (21, 22, 25, 27, 29)?

List the next two even numbers in each sequence:

2.	4,	6,	8,	...,	...
3.	22,	24,	26,	...,	...
4.	34,	36,	38,	...,	...
5.	20,	18,	16,	...,	...
6.	50,	48,	46,	...,	...
7.	60,	62,	64,	...,	...

List all the factors of

8. 5	**10.** 20	**12.** 27	**14.** 35	**16.** 42
9. 6	**11.** 25	**13.** 33	**15.** 36	**17.** 48

List the next two odd numbers in each sequence:

18.	5,	7,	9,	...,	...
19.	27,	29,	31,	...,	...
20.	41,	39,	37,	...,	...
21.	51,	53,	55,	...,	...
22.	71,	69,	67,	...,	...
23.	101,	99,	97,	...,	...

Use all the digits (4, 1, 7, 6) *once only* to write

24. the largest possible even number

25. the largest possible odd number

26. the smallest possible even number

27. the smallest possible odd number.

From the set of numbers (8, 9, 10, 11, 12, 13, 14) pick out

28. a factor of 9

29. a multiple of 6

30. the smallest prime number

31. the largest prime number.

Express the following numbers as products of prime factors:

32.	10	**34.**	15	**36.**	32	**38.**	40	**40.**	60
33.	14	**35.**	28	**37.**	36	**39.**	48	**41.**	150

42. The sum of three consecutive even numbers is 138. What are the three numbers?

43. The sum of 5 consecutive odd numbers is 105. What are the 5 numbers?

44. Which of the numbers (1, 2, 3, 4, 6, 8, 12) are not factors of 6?

Complete:

45. $2 \times 2 \times 2 \times \ldots = 24$

46. $2 \times 3 \times \ldots = 30$

47. $2 \times 2 \times 2 \times \ldots = 56$

48. $2 \times 3 \times 3 \times \ldots = 54$

49. $2 \times 5 \times \ldots = 50$

50. The sum of three consecutive whole numbers is 36. What is the smallest of these numbers?

51. Find the sum of three consecutive odd numbers if the largest one is 21.

52. Find the sum of the first six odd numbers.

Chapter Seven

Fractions

A. Equivalent fractions

The diagram shows fractions which are *equivalent:*

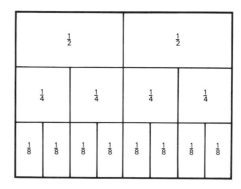

1 half $=$ 2 quarters $=$ 4 eighths

also written

$$\frac{1}{2} = \frac{2}{4} = \frac{4}{8}$$

These three fractions are called *equivalent fractions.*

To make one fraction equivalent to another fraction we can multiply both numerator and denominator by the same number; for example,

$$\frac{3}{5} = \frac{3 \times 2}{5 \times 2} = \frac{6}{10}$$

Or we can divide both numerator and denominator by the same number; for example,

$$\frac{8}{12} = \frac{8 \div 4}{12 \div 4} = \frac{2}{3}$$

Examples Put in the missing number to complete equivalent fractions:

(a) $\dfrac{2}{3} = \dfrac{}{15}$ (b) $\dfrac{3}{4} = \dfrac{9}{}$ (c) $\dfrac{}{5} = \dfrac{2}{10}$

(d) $\dfrac{6}{} = \dfrac{1}{4}$ (e) $\dfrac{2}{3} = \dfrac{2 \times}{24}$ (f) $\dfrac{3}{8} = \dfrac{9}{\times 4}$

Solutions (a) $\dfrac{2^{\times 5}}{3_{\times 5}} = \dfrac{\boxed{10}}{15}$ or $\dfrac{2}{3} = \dfrac{\boxed{10}}{15}$ 3 into 15 = 5, 5 × 2 = 10

(b) $\dfrac{3^{\times 3}}{4_{\times 3}} = \dfrac{9}{\boxed{12}}$ or $\dfrac{3}{4} = \dfrac{9}{\boxed{12}}$ 3 into 9 = 3, 3 × 4 = 12

(c) $\dfrac{\boxed{1}}{5} = \dfrac{2 \div 2}{10 \div 2}$ or $\dfrac{\boxed{1}}{5} = \dfrac{2}{10}$ 5 into 10 = 2, 2 ÷ 2 = 1

(d) $\dfrac{6}{\boxed{24}} = \dfrac{1^{\times 6}}{4_{\times 6}}$ or $\dfrac{6}{\boxed{24}} = \dfrac{1}{4}$ 1 into 6 = 6, 6 × 4 = 24

(e) $\dfrac{2^{\times 8}}{3_{\times 8}} = \dfrac{2 \times \boxed{8}}{24}$ or $\dfrac{2}{3} = \dfrac{2 \times \boxed{8}}{24}$ $\boxed{16 \div 2}$ 3 into 24 = 8,
8 × 2 = 16,
16 ÷ 2 = 8

(f) $\dfrac{3^{\times 3}}{8_{\times 3}} = \dfrac{9}{\boxed{6} \times 4}$ or $\dfrac{3}{8} = \dfrac{9}{\boxed{6} \times 4}$ $\boxed{24 \div 4}$ 3 into 9 = 3,
3 × 8 = 24,
24 ÷ 4 = 6

Exercise 1 Put a number in the empty space to make an equivalent fraction:

1. $\dfrac{1}{3} = \dfrac{}{15}$ 5. $\dfrac{5}{6} = \dfrac{15}{}$ 9. $\dfrac{8}{} = \dfrac{2}{3}$

2. $\dfrac{2}{5} = \dfrac{4}{}$ 6. $\dfrac{2}{3} = \dfrac{12}{}$ 10. $\dfrac{1}{5} = \dfrac{}{15}$

3. $\dfrac{3}{4} = \dfrac{6}{}$ 7. $\dfrac{}{3} = \dfrac{12}{36}$ 11. $\dfrac{3}{10} = \dfrac{}{30}$

4. $\dfrac{7}{10} = \dfrac{}{50}$ 8. $\dfrac{}{2} = \dfrac{6}{12}$ 12. $\dfrac{}{4} = \dfrac{5}{20}$

13. $\dfrac{}{8} = \dfrac{15}{40}$		**19.** $\dfrac{1}{} = \dfrac{7}{14}$		**25.** $\dfrac{2}{3} = \dfrac{8}{4\times}$	
14. $\dfrac{9}{} = \dfrac{3}{5}$		**20.** $\dfrac{5}{} = \dfrac{15}{24}$		**26.** $\dfrac{3}{8} = \dfrac{\times 9}{24}$	
15. $\dfrac{10}{} = \dfrac{2}{5}$		**21.** $\dfrac{1}{3} = \dfrac{3\times}{18}$		**27.** $\dfrac{5}{6} = \dfrac{\times 5}{30}$	
16. $\dfrac{16}{100} = \dfrac{}{25}$		**22.** $\dfrac{3}{10} = \dfrac{2\times}{60}$		**28.** $\dfrac{2}{3} = \dfrac{\times 3}{18}$	
17. $\dfrac{10}{35} = \dfrac{}{7}$		**23.** $\dfrac{3}{5} = \dfrac{\times 4}{20}$		**29.** $\dfrac{2}{5} = \dfrac{8}{2\times}$	
18. $\dfrac{}{5} = \dfrac{20}{25}$		**24.** $\dfrac{3}{4} = \dfrac{24}{2\times}$		**30.** $\dfrac{1}{4} = \dfrac{8}{16\times}$	

B. Cancelling

To cancel a fraction means to reduce it to lowest terms.

Look at the fraction $\dfrac{12}{30}$.

Question: What number can divide *both* numerator and denominator?

Answer: 1, 2, 3 and 6.

Question: Which is the biggest number that can divide both numerator and denominator?

Answer: 6

So that to reduce $\dfrac{12}{30}$ to lowest terms we divide *both* 12 and 30 by 6:

$$\frac{\overset{2}{\cancel{12}}}{\underset{5}{\cancel{30}}} = \frac{2}{5}$$

Remember that the number 1 is never used to cancel fractions.

Examples   Cancel these fractions: **(a)** $\dfrac{15}{20}$ **(b)** $\dfrac{16}{24}$

Solutions   **(a)** $\dfrac{\overset{3}{\cancel{15}}}{\underset{4}{\cancel{20}}} = \dfrac{3}{4}$

(We divide both 15 and 20 by 5)

(b) $\dfrac{\overset{2}{\cancel{16}}}{\underset{3}{\cancel{24}}} = \dfrac{2}{3}$

(We divide both 16 and 24 by 8)

Exercise 2 Reduce the following fractions to lowest terms:

1. $\dfrac{5}{10}$	**9.** $\dfrac{9}{30}$	**17.** $\dfrac{36}{45}$	**25.** $\dfrac{6}{54}$
2. $\dfrac{6}{8}$	**10.** $\dfrac{15}{25}$	**18.** $\dfrac{22}{55}$	**26.** $\dfrac{20}{50}$
3. $\dfrac{4}{12}$	**11.** $\dfrac{16}{24}$	**19.** $\dfrac{30}{75}$	**27.** $\dfrac{36}{54}$
4. $\dfrac{6}{15}$	**12.** $\dfrac{12}{20}$	**20.** $\dfrac{32}{48}$	**28.** $\dfrac{15}{75}$
5. $\dfrac{8}{20}$	**13.** $\dfrac{16}{40}$	**21.** $\dfrac{24}{60}$	**29.** $\dfrac{25}{100}$
6. $\dfrac{10}{15}$	**14.** $\dfrac{28}{40}$	**22.** $\dfrac{21}{63}$	**30.** $\dfrac{75}{100}$
7. $\dfrac{12}{18}$	**15.** $\dfrac{27}{36}$	**23.** $\dfrac{5}{100}$	
8. $\dfrac{14}{21}$	**16.** $\dfrac{9}{27}$	**24.** $\dfrac{34}{40}$	

C. Mixed numbers and improper fractions

The diagram shows
1 whole + 1 quarter (shaded)

Also written $1\dfrac{1}{4} = \dfrac{5}{4}$

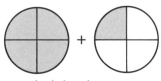

1 whole + 1 quarter
or 4 quarters + 1 quarter

$1\dfrac{1}{4}$ is called a *mixed number*. Any whole number plus a fraction is called a mixed number.

The fraction $\dfrac{5}{4}$ is called an *improper fraction*. Any fraction where the numerator is greater than the denominator is called an improper fraction.

1. Changing mixed numbers to improper fractions

Examples   (a) $2\frac{2}{3} = \frac{2 \times 3 + 2}{3} = \frac{8}{3}$

(b) $5\frac{1}{2} = \frac{5 \times 2 + 1}{2} = \frac{11}{2}$

Exercise 3   Change the following mixed numbers to improper fractions:

1. $1\frac{1}{2}$	**6.** $5\frac{2}{5}$	**11.** $7\frac{1}{2}$	**16.** $8\frac{3}{5}$
2. $2\frac{3}{4}$	**7.** $1\frac{2}{3}$	**12.** $10\frac{2}{3}$	**17.** $7\frac{1}{8}$
3. $4\frac{1}{3}$	**8.** $2\frac{3}{8}$	**13.** $6\frac{5}{8}$	**18.** $12\frac{5}{12}$
4. $3\frac{1}{2}$	**9.** $6\frac{1}{4}$	**14.** $2\frac{2}{5}$	**19.** $11\frac{1}{3}$
5. $4\frac{3}{4}$	**10.** $5\frac{3}{8}$	**15.** $4\frac{5}{6}$	**20.** $4\frac{7}{9}$

2. Changing improper fractions to mixed numbers

Examples   (a) $\frac{15}{4} = 15 \div 4 = 3 + 3 \text{ quarters} = 3\frac{3}{4}$

(b) $\frac{20}{3} = 20 \div 3 = 6 + 2 \text{ thirds} = 6\frac{2}{3}$

Exercise 4   Change the following improper fractions to mixed numbers:

1. $\frac{7}{3}$	**6.** $\frac{19}{2}$	**11.** $\frac{39}{9}$	**16.** $\frac{60}{11}$
2. $\frac{9}{5}$	**7.** $\frac{27}{6}$	**12.** $\frac{41}{6}$	**17.** $\frac{37}{10}$
3. $\frac{10}{3}$	**8.** $\frac{40}{7}$	**13.** $\frac{19}{10}$	**18.** $\frac{47}{11}$
4. $\frac{15}{4}$	**9.** $\frac{18}{5}$	**14.** $\frac{27}{7}$	**19.** $\frac{41}{12}$
5. $\frac{9}{2}$	**10.** $\frac{22}{5}$	**15.** $\frac{40}{3}$	**20.** $\frac{15}{8}$

D. Addition and subtraction of fractions

1. Fractions having the same denominators

The diagram shows three
quarters plus three quarters:
3 quarters + 3 quarters
= 6 quarters
also written

$$\frac{3}{4} + \frac{3}{4} = \frac{3+3}{4} = \frac{6}{4} = \frac{3}{2}$$
$$= 1\frac{1}{2}$$

Note that we only add the two numerators.

Examples Find: (a) $\frac{5}{6} - \frac{1}{6}$ (b) $\frac{7}{8} + \frac{3}{8}$ (c) $1\frac{2}{5} + 1\frac{4}{5}$ (d) $2\frac{1}{4} - 1\frac{3}{4}$

Solutions

(a) $\dfrac{5}{6} - \dfrac{1}{6} = \dfrac{5-1}{6} = \dfrac{4}{6} = \dfrac{2}{3}$

(b) $\dfrac{7}{8} + \dfrac{3}{8} = \dfrac{7+3}{8} = \dfrac{10}{8} = \dfrac{5}{4} = 1\dfrac{1}{4}$

(c) $1\dfrac{2}{5} + 1\dfrac{4}{5} = 2 + \dfrac{2+4}{5} = 2 + \dfrac{6}{5} = 2 + 1\dfrac{1}{5} = 3\dfrac{1}{5}$

    or $1\dfrac{2}{5} + 1\dfrac{4}{5} = \dfrac{7}{5} + \dfrac{9}{5} = \dfrac{7+9}{5} = \dfrac{16}{5} = 3\dfrac{1}{5}$

(d) $2\dfrac{1}{4} - 1\dfrac{3}{4} = \dfrac{9}{4} - \dfrac{7}{4} = \dfrac{9-7}{4} = \dfrac{2}{4} = \dfrac{1}{2}$

Exercise 5 Find:

1. $\dfrac{7}{8} - \dfrac{1}{8}$

2. $\dfrac{3}{4} - \dfrac{1}{4}$

3. $\dfrac{1}{6} + \dfrac{1}{6}$

4. $\dfrac{7}{12} - \dfrac{5}{12}$

5. $\dfrac{7}{10} + \dfrac{1}{10}$

6. $\dfrac{2}{5} + \dfrac{3}{5}$

7. $\dfrac{2}{3} + \dfrac{2}{3}$ 12. $3\dfrac{1}{4} + 1\dfrac{3}{4}$ 17. $1\dfrac{1}{6} + \dfrac{5}{6}$

8. $\dfrac{9}{10} - \dfrac{7}{10}$ 13. $1\dfrac{1}{5} + 2\dfrac{2}{5}$ 18. $2\dfrac{4}{5} + \dfrac{3}{5}$

9. $\dfrac{11}{12} - \dfrac{5}{12}$ 14. $3\dfrac{1}{3} - 2\dfrac{1}{3}$ 19. $3\dfrac{1}{3} - 2\dfrac{2}{3}$

10. $\dfrac{14}{15} - \dfrac{7}{15}$ 15. $4\dfrac{1}{4} - 1\dfrac{3}{4}$ 20. $4\dfrac{1}{5} - 2\dfrac{3}{5}$

11. $1\dfrac{1}{2} + 2\dfrac{1}{2}$ 16. $1\dfrac{3}{8} - \dfrac{7}{8}$

2. Fractions having different denominators

Examples Find: (a) $\dfrac{2}{3} + \dfrac{3}{4}$ (c) $1\dfrac{1}{2} + 1\dfrac{3}{4}$ (e) $5 - 1\dfrac{2}{3}$

(b) $\dfrac{3}{5} - \dfrac{2}{10}$ (d) $2\dfrac{1}{2} - \dfrac{3}{4}$

Solutions (a)

$$\dfrac{2}{3} + \dfrac{3}{4}$$

*L.C.D. is 12, $= \dfrac{8 + 9}{12}$

$$= \dfrac{17}{12}$$

$$= 1\dfrac{5}{12}$$

(b)

$$\dfrac{3}{5} - \dfrac{2}{10}$$

L.C.D. is 10, $= \dfrac{6 - 2}{10}$

$$= \dfrac{4}{10}$$

$$= \dfrac{2}{5}$$

(c)

$$1\dfrac{1}{2} + 1\dfrac{3}{4} \qquad or \qquad 1\dfrac{1}{2} + 1\dfrac{3}{4}$$

L.C.D. is 4, $= 1 + 1 + \dfrac{2 + 3}{4} \qquad\qquad = \dfrac{3}{2} + \dfrac{7}{4}$

$$= 2\dfrac{5}{4} \qquad\qquad\qquad = \dfrac{6 + 7}{4}$$

$$= 2 + 1\dfrac{1}{4} \qquad\qquad\quad = \dfrac{13}{4}$$

$$= 3\dfrac{1}{4} \qquad\qquad\qquad = 3\dfrac{1}{4}$$

*L.C.D. stands for lowest common denominator.

(d)
$$2\frac{1}{2} - \frac{3}{4}$$
$$= \frac{5}{2} - \frac{3}{4}$$
L.C.D. is 4, $= \dfrac{10-3}{4}$
$$= \frac{7}{4}$$
$$= 1\frac{3}{4}$$

(e)
$$5 - 1\frac{2}{3}$$
$$= \frac{5}{1} - \frac{5}{3}$$
L.C.D. is 3, $= \dfrac{15-5}{3}$
$$= \frac{10}{3}$$
$$= 3\frac{1}{3}$$

Exercise 6 Find:

1. $\dfrac{5}{6} - \dfrac{2}{3}$
2. $\dfrac{5}{6} + \dfrac{2}{3}$
3. $\dfrac{3}{4} - \dfrac{1}{2}$
4. $\dfrac{3}{4} + \dfrac{1}{2}$
5. $\dfrac{7}{8} - \dfrac{1}{2}$
6. $\dfrac{7}{8} + \dfrac{1}{2}$
7. $\dfrac{3}{4} - \dfrac{3}{8}$

8. $\dfrac{3}{4} + \dfrac{3}{8}$
9. $\dfrac{7}{10} - \dfrac{1}{2}$
10. $\dfrac{7}{10} + \dfrac{1}{2}$
11. $\dfrac{1}{2} - \dfrac{1}{3}$
12. $\dfrac{1}{2} + \dfrac{1}{3}$
13. $\dfrac{3}{4} - \dfrac{2}{3}$
14. $\dfrac{3}{4} + \dfrac{2}{3}$

15. $\dfrac{1}{2} - \dfrac{1}{10}$
16. $\dfrac{1}{2} + \dfrac{1}{10}$
17. $\dfrac{1}{2} + \dfrac{2}{5}$
18. $\dfrac{1}{2} - \dfrac{2}{5}$
19. $\dfrac{3}{4} - \dfrac{7}{12}$
20. $\dfrac{3}{4} + \dfrac{7}{12}$

21. $6 - 1\frac{2}{3}$
22. $1 - \dfrac{3}{4}$
23. $2 - 1\frac{1}{2}$
24. $5 - \dfrac{3}{8}$
25. $6 - 2\frac{1}{5}$

26. $\dfrac{5}{6} + \dfrac{3}{4}$
27. $\dfrac{3}{8} + \dfrac{1}{6}$
28. $1\frac{1}{2} + 1\frac{1}{3}$
29. $2\frac{1}{2} - 1\frac{1}{6}$
30. $1\frac{7}{10} + 1\frac{4}{5}$

31. $1\frac{3}{5} - \dfrac{7}{8}$
32. $2\frac{1}{4} - 1\frac{5}{6}$
33. $\dfrac{1}{2} + \dfrac{2}{5} + \dfrac{3}{10}$
34. $\dfrac{1}{3} + \dfrac{1}{2} + \dfrac{1}{4}$
35. $\dfrac{7}{12} + \dfrac{1}{6} + \dfrac{1}{3}$

E. Multiplication of fractions

Examples Find: **(a)** $\frac{3}{4} \times \frac{1}{2}$ **(b)** $\frac{3}{4} \times \frac{2}{3}$ **(c)** $10 \times \frac{3}{5}$ **(d)** $3\frac{3}{4} \times 1\frac{1}{5}$

Solutions **(a)** $\frac{3}{4} \times \frac{1}{2} = \frac{3 \times 1}{4 \times 2} = \frac{3}{8}$

(b) $\frac{3}{4} \times \frac{2}{3} = \frac{3 \times 2}{4 \times 3} = \frac{\overset{1}{\cancel{6}}}{\underset{2}{\cancel{12}}} = \frac{1}{2}$

In example **(b)** it would have been easier to cancel first and then multiply like this: $\frac{\overset{1}{\cancel{3}}}{\underset{2}{\cancel{4}}} \times \frac{\overset{1}{\cancel{2}}}{\underset{1}{\cancel{3}}} = \frac{1 \times 1}{2 \times 1} = \frac{1}{2}$

(c) $10 \times \frac{3}{5} = \frac{\overset{2}{\cancel{10}}}{1} \times \frac{3}{\underset{1}{\cancel{5}}} = \frac{2 \times 3}{1 \times 1} = \frac{6}{1} = 6$

(d) $3\frac{3}{4} \times 1\frac{1}{5} = \frac{\overset{3}{\cancel{15}}}{\underset{2}{\cancel{4}}} \times \frac{\overset{3}{\cancel{6}}}{\underset{1}{\cancel{5}}} = \frac{3 \times 3}{2 \times 1} = \frac{9}{2} = 4\frac{1}{2}$

Exercise 7 Find:

1. $\frac{1}{2} \times \frac{1}{4}$ **10.** $\frac{3}{4} \times \frac{4}{5}$ **19.** $\frac{8}{9} \times \frac{3}{4}$

2. $\frac{2}{5} \times \frac{1}{3}$ **11.** $\frac{1}{3} \times \frac{3}{4}$ **20.** $\frac{4}{5} \times \frac{5}{8}$

3. $\frac{2}{3} \times \frac{4}{5}$ **12.** $\frac{5}{9} \times \frac{4}{5}$ **21.** $4 \times \frac{2}{3}$

4. $\frac{3}{8} \times \frac{1}{2}$ **13.** $\frac{3}{15} \times \frac{2}{3}$ **22.** $8 \times \frac{3}{4}$

5. $\frac{2}{5} \times \frac{2}{3}$ **14.** $\frac{1}{3} \times \frac{3}{5}$ **23.** $2 \times \frac{1}{2}$

6. $\frac{2}{3} \times \frac{5}{8}$ **15.** $\frac{3}{5} \times \frac{5}{8}$ **24.** $2 \times \frac{2}{5}$

7. $\frac{3}{10} \times \frac{5}{8}$ **16.** $\frac{2}{5} \times \frac{5}{6}$ **25.** $5 \times \frac{3}{4}$

8. $\frac{5}{6} \times \frac{3}{8}$ **17.** $\frac{3}{8} \times \frac{4}{15}$ **26.** $\frac{3}{4} \times 6$

9. $\frac{1}{4} \times \frac{6}{15}$ **18.** $\frac{2}{3} \times \frac{3}{4}$ **27.** $\frac{2}{5} \times 20$

28. $\frac{1}{3} \times 12$ **34.** $3\frac{1}{5} \times 3\frac{3}{4}$ **40.** $2\frac{2}{3} \times 1\frac{7}{8}$

29. $\frac{5}{8} \times 10$ **35.** $\frac{3}{16} \times 1\frac{2}{3}$ **41.** $\frac{2}{3} \times \frac{3}{8} \times \frac{4}{5}$

30. $\frac{5}{6} \times 8$ **36.** $\frac{3}{8} \times 3\frac{1}{3}$ **42.** $\frac{1}{2} \times \frac{3}{10} \times \frac{5}{6}$

31. $1\frac{1}{2} \times \frac{2}{5}$ **37.** $1\frac{3}{4} \times 2\frac{2}{7}$ **43.** $\frac{1}{3} \times \frac{3}{4} \times \frac{1}{2}$

32. $5\frac{1}{3} \times \frac{3}{4}$ **38.** $3\frac{1}{3} \times 2\frac{2}{5}$ **44.** $\frac{3}{5} \times \frac{5}{12} \times \frac{1}{2}$

33. $4\frac{2}{3} \times 2\frac{1}{2}$ **39.** $1\frac{7}{8} \times 1\frac{1}{3}$ **45.** $1\frac{4}{5} \times \frac{5}{6} \times 1\frac{1}{3}$

F. Finding a fraction of a number, money, time, mass, etc.

In mathematics the term 'of' means to multiply.

Examples   Find: **(a)** $\frac{1}{5}$ of 10   **(b)** $\frac{2}{3}$ of \$60

(c) $\frac{3}{10}$ of 1 kg   **(d)** $\frac{3}{4}$ of 100 m

Solutions   **(a)** $\frac{1}{5}$ of $10 = \frac{1}{\overset{}{\underset{1}{\cancel{5}}}} \times \frac{\overset{2}{\cancel{10}}}{1} = \frac{2 \times 1}{1 \times 1} = \frac{2}{1} = 2$

(b) $\frac{2}{3}$ of $\$60 = \frac{2}{\underset{1}{\cancel{3}}} \times \frac{\overset{20}{\cancel{\$60}}}{1} = \frac{2 \times \$20}{1 \times 1} = \frac{\$40}{1} = \$40$

(c) $\frac{3}{10}$ of $1\,\text{kg} = \frac{3}{\underset{1}{\cancel{10}}} \times \frac{\overset{100}{\cancel{1000}}}{1}\,\text{g} = \frac{3 \times 100}{1 \times 1}\,\text{g} = \frac{300}{1}\,\text{g}$

$= 300\,\text{g}$

(d) $\frac{3}{4}$ of $100\,\text{m} = \frac{3}{\underset{1}{\cancel{4}}} \times \frac{\overset{25}{\cancel{100}}}{1}\,\text{m} = \frac{3 \times 25}{1 \times 1}\,\text{m} = \frac{75}{1}\,\text{m}$

$= 75\,\text{m}$

Exercise 8 Find:

1. $\frac{1}{2}$ of 30

2. $\frac{1}{4}$ of 24

3. $\frac{1}{3}$ of 15

4. $\frac{2}{3}$ of 24

5. $\frac{3}{5}$ of 20

6. $\frac{1}{2}$ of $10

7. $\frac{3}{10}$ of $50

8. $\frac{5}{6}$ of $30

9. $\frac{7}{8}$ of $40

10. $\frac{3}{8}$ of $240

11. $\frac{2}{5}$ of 60 g

12. $\frac{1}{3}$ of 24 L

13. $\frac{3}{10}$ of 200 m

14. $\frac{5}{6}$ of 120 kg

15. $\frac{1}{4}$ of 500 g

16. $\frac{2}{3}$ of 150 cm

17. $\frac{1}{2}$ of 1 min (Give the answer in seconds)

18. $\frac{3}{4}$ of 1 h (Give the answer in minutes)

19. $\frac{7}{10}$ of 40 km

20. $\frac{5}{12}$ of $240

G. Division of fractions

The diagrams show a half divided by both 2 and 4:

Notice that $\dfrac{1}{2} \div 2 = \dfrac{1}{4}$

and $\qquad \dfrac{1}{2} \div 4 = \dfrac{1}{8}$

So that $\qquad \dfrac{1}{2} \div 2$ implies that $\dfrac{1}{2} \times \dfrac{1}{2} = \dfrac{1}{4}$

and $\qquad \dfrac{1}{2} \div 4$ implies that $\dfrac{1}{2} \times \dfrac{1}{4} = \dfrac{1}{8}$

To divide by a number is the same as to multiply by the inverse of that number. The inverse of 2 is $\dfrac{1}{2}$, the inverse of 4 is $\dfrac{1}{4}$ and the inverse of $\dfrac{1}{6}$ is $\dfrac{6}{1}$, etc.

Examples   Find: (a) $\dfrac{3}{4} \div \dfrac{1}{4}$ (b) $6 \div \dfrac{2}{3}$ (c) $2\dfrac{2}{3} \div 2$

(d) $3\dfrac{1}{2} \div 1\dfrac{1}{4}$

Solutions   (a) $\dfrac{3}{4} \div \dfrac{1}{4} = \dfrac{3}{\overset{1}{\cancel{4}}} \times \dfrac{\overset{1}{\cancel{4}}}{1} = \dfrac{3 \times 1}{1 \times 1} = \dfrac{3}{1} = 3$

(b) $6 \div \dfrac{2}{3} = \dfrac{\overset{3}{\cancel{6}}}{1} \times \dfrac{3}{\underset{1}{\cancel{2}}} = \dfrac{3 \times 3}{1 \times 1} = \dfrac{9}{1} = 9$

(c) $2\dfrac{2}{3} \div 2 = \dfrac{8}{3} \div \dfrac{2}{1} = \dfrac{\overset{4}{\cancel{8}}}{3} \times \dfrac{1}{\underset{1}{\cancel{2}}} = \dfrac{4 \times 1}{3 \times 1} = \dfrac{4}{3} = 1\dfrac{1}{3}$

(d) $3\dfrac{1}{2} \div 1\dfrac{1}{4} = \dfrac{7}{2} \div \dfrac{5}{4} = \dfrac{7}{\underset{1}{\cancel{2}}} \times \dfrac{\overset{2}{\cancel{4}}}{5} = \dfrac{7 \times 2}{1 \times 5} = \dfrac{14}{5} = 2\dfrac{4}{5}$

Note that only the term that comes *after* the division sign is inverted.

Exercise 9   Find:

1. $\dfrac{1}{4} \div \dfrac{1}{3}$ 4. $\dfrac{1}{4} \div \dfrac{1}{2}$ 7. $\dfrac{5}{6} \div \dfrac{2}{3}$

2. $\dfrac{7}{8} \div \dfrac{3}{4}$ 5. $\dfrac{1}{3} \div \dfrac{3}{4}$ 8. $\dfrac{7}{10} \div \dfrac{2}{5}$

3. $\dfrac{3}{5} \div \dfrac{2}{3}$ 6. $\dfrac{3}{8} \div \dfrac{1}{2}$ 9. $\dfrac{1}{2} \div \dfrac{1}{2}$

10. $\dfrac{5}{8} \div \dfrac{1}{4}$

11. $10 \div \dfrac{2}{5}$

12. $5 \div \dfrac{1}{3}$

13. $7 \div \dfrac{2}{3}$

14. $3 \div \dfrac{3}{4}$

15. $4 \div \dfrac{1}{2}$

16. $\dfrac{1}{4} \div 5$

17. $\dfrac{3}{8} \div 6$

18. $\dfrac{2}{5} \div 2$

19. $\dfrac{1}{3} \div 9$

20. $\dfrac{3}{4} \div 12$

21. $2\dfrac{1}{3} \div \dfrac{4}{15}$

22. $3\dfrac{2}{3} \div \dfrac{9}{20}$

23. $4\dfrac{1}{2} \div \dfrac{2}{3}$

24. $6\dfrac{1}{4} \div \dfrac{5}{6}$

25. $2\dfrac{2}{5} \div \dfrac{6}{15}$

26. $\dfrac{3}{10} \div 7\dfrac{1}{2}$

27. $\dfrac{3}{5} \div 1\dfrac{4}{5}$

28. $\dfrac{7}{8} \div 1\dfrac{3}{4}$

29. $\dfrac{9}{10} \div 4\dfrac{1}{5}$

30. $\dfrac{2}{5} \div 1\dfrac{2}{3}$

31. $1\dfrac{1}{3} \div 2\dfrac{2}{5}$

32. $4\dfrac{1}{2} \div 1\dfrac{1}{2}$

33. $5\dfrac{2}{5} \div 1\dfrac{4}{5}$

34. $1\dfrac{1}{4} \div 3\dfrac{1}{2}$

35. $1\dfrac{1}{3} \div 2\dfrac{1}{3}$

36. $1\dfrac{1}{2} \div 2\dfrac{3}{4}$

37. $7\dfrac{1}{3} \div 1\dfrac{5}{6}$

38. $2\dfrac{2}{7} \div 1\dfrac{3}{5}$

39. $6\dfrac{3}{8} \div 5\dfrac{2}{3}$

40. $2\dfrac{1}{6} \div 9\dfrac{3}{4}$

H. Mixed +, −, ×, ÷ and 'of', of fractions

Exercise 10 Find:

1. $\dfrac{1}{6} + \dfrac{2}{3}$

2. $\dfrac{4}{5} - \dfrac{3}{4}$

3. $\dfrac{3}{5} \times \dfrac{5}{8}$

4. $\dfrac{3}{4} \div \dfrac{1}{2}$

5. $\dfrac{1}{2}$ of 26

6. $\dfrac{5}{8} \times \dfrac{4}{15}$

7. $1\dfrac{2}{3} + 1\dfrac{3}{4}$

8. $\dfrac{1}{5}$ of 100

9. $3\dfrac{1}{3} - 2\dfrac{3}{4}$

10. $\dfrac{7}{10} \div 1\dfrac{1}{2}$

11. $\dfrac{2}{3}$ of 60 min

12. $\dfrac{3}{4}$ of $40

13. $1\dfrac{5}{8} - \dfrac{5}{6}$

14. $4\dfrac{1}{2} \times 3\dfrac{1}{5}$

15. $\dfrac{2}{3}$ of 60 g

16. $1\frac{1}{2} \times 2\frac{2}{3}$ **18.** $\frac{5}{6} \div 5$ **20.** $\frac{3}{4} + \frac{2}{3}$

17. $3\frac{3}{4} \times 1\frac{1}{5}$ **19.** $6 \div 1\frac{1}{3}$

21. $\frac{5}{8} - \frac{1}{4}$ **23.** $1\frac{1}{2} + 2\frac{7}{8}$ **25.** $2\frac{4}{5} \div 2\frac{1}{10}$

22. $2\frac{1}{3} - 1\frac{3}{4}$ **24.** $\frac{7}{8} + \frac{1}{2}$

I. Problems involving fractions

Example   A farmer had 240 birds. $\frac{1}{3}$ of them were chickens, $\frac{1}{4}$ were turkeys and the rest were ducks. What fraction were ducks? How many ducks were there?

Solution

$$\text{Fraction of chickens + fraction of turkeys} = \frac{1}{3} + \frac{1}{4}$$
$$= \frac{4+3}{12}$$
$$= \frac{7}{12}$$

$$\text{Fraction of ducks} = 1 - \frac{7}{12}$$
$$= \frac{1}{1} - \frac{7}{12}$$
$$= \frac{12-7}{12}$$
$$= \frac{5}{12}$$

$$\text{Number of ducks} = \frac{5}{12} \text{ of } 240$$
$$= \frac{5}{12} \times \frac{240}{1}$$
$$= 100$$

Exercise 11

1. Last Saturday Mary had $15 for pocket money. She spent $\frac{1}{3}$ of it at the snackette and put the rest in her savings box. **(a)** How much did she spend? **(b)** How much did she put in her savings box?

2. Out of 100 cherries, $\frac{2}{5}$ were bad. How many cherries were good?

3. At a certain Composite school there were 480 pupils. $\frac{1}{3}$ of them were infants, $\frac{5}{12}$ were juniors and the rest were seniors. **(a)** What fraction were seniors? **(b)** How many pupils were infants? **(c)** How many pupils were juniors? **(d)** How many pupils were seniors?

4. Ann had a bar of chocolate. She gave $\frac{1}{4}$ of it to Suzie and $\frac{1}{8}$ to Ruth. What fraction did she have left?

5. Mother had a crate of 30 eggs. For breakfast she boiled $\frac{1}{3}$ of them and fried $\frac{1}{6}$. **(a)** What fraction of eggs had she left? **(b)** How many eggs did she boil? **(c)** How many eggs did she fry? **(d)** How many eggs were left?

6. If $\frac{1}{3}$ of a number is 12, what is the number?

7. $\frac{1}{5}$ of the money in my purse is $5.00. How much money do I have in my purse?

8. There are 24 teachers at our school. One day $\frac{1}{6}$ of them were absent from school and $\frac{1}{8}$ of them were out on school business. **(a)** What fraction of teachers were present? **(b)** How many teachers were present? **(c)** How many teachers were absent?

9. $\frac{2}{3}$ of the houses in our village have telephones. If there are 60 houses in our village, how many of them do not have telephones?

10. A small farmer had 12 acres of land. On Monday he ploughed $\frac{1}{3}$ of it and on Tuesday he ploughed $\frac{1}{4}$. **(a)** What fraction of land remained unploughed? **(b)** How many acres of land remained unploughed?

J. Ordering fractions

To *order* fractions means to arrange the fractions in order of size, either beginning with the smallest first or beginning with the largest first.

If fractions have the *same numerator,* the fraction with the biggest denominator is the smallest fraction.

Example   Arrange these fractions in order of size, smallest first:

$$\frac{1}{5}, \quad \frac{1}{3}, \quad \frac{1}{4}, \quad \frac{1}{6}$$

Solution $\frac{1}{6}, \quad \frac{1}{5}, \quad \frac{1}{4}, \quad \frac{1}{3}$

If fractions have the *same denominator,* the fraction with the smallest numerator is the smallest fraction.

Example   Arrange these fractions in order of size, smallest first:

$$\frac{1}{5}, \quad \frac{4}{5}, \quad \frac{3}{5}, \quad \frac{2}{5}$$

Solution $\frac{1}{5}, \quad \frac{2}{5}, \quad \frac{3}{5}, \quad \frac{4}{5}$

If fractions have different numerators *and* different denominators, they need to be changed to ones having the same denominator. To do this, we find the L.C.M. of the denominators.

Example   Arrange these fractions in order of size, smallest first:

$$\frac{1}{6}, \quad \frac{3}{4}, \quad \frac{2}{3}, \quad \frac{7}{12}$$

Solution   Changing the denominators:

$$\frac{2}{12}, \frac{9}{12}, \frac{8}{12}, \frac{7}{12}$$

New fractions in order of size:

$$\frac{2}{12}, \frac{7}{12}, \frac{8}{12}, \frac{9}{12}$$

Original fractions in order of size:

$$\frac{1}{6}, \frac{7}{12}, \frac{2}{3}, \frac{3}{4}$$

Exercise 12 Arrange the fractions in each question in order of size, smallest first:

1. $\dfrac{3}{8}, \dfrac{1}{8}, \dfrac{7}{8}, \dfrac{5}{8}$

2. $\dfrac{5}{10}, \dfrac{3}{10}, \dfrac{7}{10}, \dfrac{1}{10}$

3. $\dfrac{7}{12}, \dfrac{3}{12}, \dfrac{5}{12}, \dfrac{11}{12}$

4. $\dfrac{3}{5}, \dfrac{3}{8}, \dfrac{3}{4}, \dfrac{3}{10}$

5. $\dfrac{1}{9}, \dfrac{1}{10}, \dfrac{1}{3}, \dfrac{1}{5}$

6. $\dfrac{5}{6}, \dfrac{5}{12}, \dfrac{5}{8}, \dfrac{5}{10}$

7. $\dfrac{5}{6}, \dfrac{2}{3}, \dfrac{7}{12}, \dfrac{1}{4}$

8. $\dfrac{1}{2}, \dfrac{3}{5}, \dfrac{7}{10}, \dfrac{11}{20}$

9. $\dfrac{9}{16}, \dfrac{5}{8}, \dfrac{3}{4}, \dfrac{1}{2}$

10. $\dfrac{3}{4}, \dfrac{2}{3}, \dfrac{9}{12}, \dfrac{5}{6}$

Chapter Eight

Decimals

A. Place value

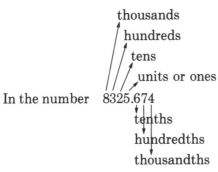

In the number   8325.674

thousands
hundreds
tens
units or ones
tenths
hundredths
thousandths

the figures before the decimal point represent units, tens, hundreds and thousands.

The first figure after the decimal point represents tenths.

The second figure after the decimal point represents hundredths.

The third figure after the decimal point represents thousandths.

So 0.6   = 6 tenths

0.67   = 67 hundredths

0.674 = 674 thousandths

Exercise 1   Complete the following. In the number 5.619:

1. 5 = 5 . . .   **3.** 6 = 6 . . .

2. 9 = 9 . . .   **4.** 1 = 1 . . .

Write a decimal point in each of the following numbers so that 6 has the value of 6 ones:

5. 6143   **6.** 2516   **7.** 9360   **8.** 8607

In the following numbers what is the value of each figure underlined?

9. 3.14̲2   **11.** 3̲9.21   **13.** 295.06̲3 **15.** 315.4̲8

10. 17̲.618   **12.** 0.62̲5   **14.** 25.18̲0 **16.** 9̲274.638

Write a decimal point in each of the following numbers so that the 4 has the value of 4 hundredths.

17. 17204   **18.** 75431   **19.** 6427   **20.** 51048

In the number 4315.278 write down the figure that represents

21. tens   **23.** tenths

22. hundredths   **24.** thousandths

B. Writing decimals as fractions or mixed numbers

Look again at the number 8325.674

where 0.6   = 6 tenths = $\frac{6}{10}$

0.67 = 67 hundredths = $\frac{67}{100}$

0.674 = 674 thousandths = $\frac{674}{1000}$

Notice that when there is *one* figure after the decimal point, the equivalent fraction has *one* zero in the denominator:
$0.6 = \frac{6}{10}$, 1 zero

When there are *two* figures after the decimal point, the equivalent fraction has *two* zeros in the denominator:
$0.67 = \frac{67}{100}$, 2 zeros.

When there are *three* figures after the decimal point, the equivalent fraction has *three* zeros in the denominator:
$0.674 = \frac{674}{1000}$, 3 zeros.

Examples   Write the following decimals as fractions or mixed numbers:

(a) 0.3   (b) 0.18   (c) 0.027   (d) 3.09

Solutions   (a) $0.3 = \dfrac{3}{10}$ (b) $0.18 = \dfrac{18}{100}$

(c) $0.027 = \dfrac{27}{1000}$ (d) $3.09 = 3\dfrac{9}{100}$

Exercise 2   Write the following as fractions or mixed numbers:

1.	0.7	**11.**	0.08	**21.**	12.8
2.	0.9	**12.**	0.93	**22.**	0.04
3.	0.013	**13.**	0.5	**23.**	2.7
4.	0.05	**14.**	0.139	**24.**	0.43
5.	3.4	**15.**	8.975	**25.**	1.09
6.	0.87	**16.**	27.9	**26.**	8.71
7.	13.01	**17.**	0.47	**27.**	4.75
8.	0.125	**18.**	0.93	**28.**	0.003
9.	0.2	**19.**	0.03	**29.**	0.165
10.	0.70	**20.**	5.6	**30.**	0.19

C. Writing fractions or mixed numbers as decimals

Examples   Write the following fractions or mixed numbers as decimals:

(a) $3\dfrac{1}{10}$ (b) $\dfrac{18}{100}$

(c) $\dfrac{15}{1000}$ (d) $17\dfrac{3}{100}$

Solutions   (a) $3\dfrac{1}{10} = 3.1$ (one zero in 10, so one figure is placed after the decimal point)

(b) $\dfrac{18}{100} = 0.18$ (two zeros in 100, so two figures are placed after the decimal point)

(c) $\dfrac{15}{1000} = 0.015$ (three zeros in 1000, so three figures are placed after the decimal point)

(d) $17\dfrac{3}{100} = 17.03$ (two zeros in 100, so two figures are placed after the decimal point)

Exercise 3   Write the following fractions or mixed numbers as decimals:

1. $\dfrac{9}{10}$		**11.** $3\dfrac{271}{1000}$		**21.** $1\dfrac{18}{1000}$	
2. $\dfrac{2}{10}$		**12.** $\dfrac{625}{1000}$		**22.** $\dfrac{3}{1000}$	
3. $5\dfrac{7}{10}$		**13.** $\dfrac{3}{10}$		**23.** $\dfrac{19}{100}$	
4. $\dfrac{11}{100}$		**14.** $\dfrac{70}{100}$		**24.** $10\dfrac{1}{100}$	
5. $\dfrac{13}{1000}$		**15.** $4\dfrac{8}{1000}$		**25.** $\dfrac{7}{1000}$	
6. $\dfrac{1}{10}$		**16.** $16\dfrac{1}{10}$		**26.** $176\dfrac{3}{10}$	
7. $8\dfrac{17}{100}$		**17.** $\dfrac{4}{100}$		**27.** $5\dfrac{4}{100}$	
8. $\dfrac{129}{1000}$		**18.** $\dfrac{13}{1000}$		**28.** $\dfrac{27}{100}$	
9. $28\dfrac{1}{10}$		**19.** $4\dfrac{9}{10}$		**29.** $\dfrac{3}{100}$	
10. $\dfrac{5}{100}$		**20.** $16\dfrac{7}{100}$		**30.** $14\dfrac{19}{100}$	

D. Writing vulgar fractions as decimals

Examples   Change the following vulgar fractions to decimals:

(a) $\dfrac{4}{5}$ (b) $\dfrac{16}{25}$ (c) $\dfrac{7}{8}$

Solutions   (a) $\dfrac{4}{5}$ means $4 \div 5$

$$\dfrac{4}{5} = 0.8$$

$$5\overline{\smash{\big)}\,4.0}$$
$$\underline{0.8}$$

(b) $\dfrac{16}{25}$ means $16 \div 25$

$$\dfrac{16}{25} = 0.64$$

$$\begin{array}{r} 0.64 \\ 25\overline{\smash{\big)}\,16.00} \\ -\underline{15\,0} \\ 0100 \\ -\underline{100} \\ 000 \end{array}$$

(c) $\dfrac{7}{8}$ means $7 \div 8$

$\dfrac{7}{8} = 0.875$

$$8\overline{)7.000}$$
$$0.875$$

Exercise 4 Change the following fractions to decimals:

1. $\dfrac{2}{5}$		**6.** $\dfrac{11}{20}$		**11.** $\dfrac{3}{4}$		**16.** $\dfrac{3}{25}$
2. $\dfrac{3}{5}$		**7.** $\dfrac{3}{20}$		**12.** $\dfrac{1}{4}$		**17.** $\dfrac{7}{25}$
3. $\dfrac{1}{5}$		**8.** $\dfrac{13}{20}$		**13.** $\dfrac{1}{8}$		**18.** $\dfrac{9}{25}$
4. $\dfrac{7}{20}$		**9.** $\dfrac{17}{20}$		**14.** $\dfrac{3}{8}$		**19.** $\dfrac{11}{25}$
5. $\dfrac{9}{20}$		**10.** $\dfrac{19}{20}$		**15.** $\dfrac{5}{8}$		**20.** $\dfrac{18}{25}$

E. Addition and subtraction of decimals

1. Addition of decimals

Examples Set down the following vertically and add them up, keeping the decimal points directly underneath each other:

(a) $6.81 + 4.7$ **(b)** $9.173 + 3.87 + 0.6$

Solutions **(a)** $6.81 + 4.7$
$= 6.81 + 4.70$
$= 11.51$

$$6.81$$
$$4.70$$
$$\overline{11.51}$$

Note that one zero is added to 4.7 so that it now has the same number of figures after the decimal point as 6.81.

(b) $9.173 + 3.87 + 0.6$
$= 9.173 + 3.870 + 0.600$
$= 13.643$

$$9.173$$
$$3.870$$
$$0.600$$
$$\overline{13.643}$$

Note that 9.173 has three figures after the decimal point. One zero is added to 3.87 and two zeros are added to 0.6 so that these two numbers now have the same number of figures after the decimal point as 9.173.

Exercise 5 Copy the following and work them out:

1.	2.8	**5.**	8.54	**9.**	6.73	
	+ 7.1		+ 0.75		2.40	
	———		———		+ 1.38	
					———	
2.	3.5	**6.**	7.25			
	+ 8.3		+ 3.99	**10.**	63.60	
	———		———		8.47	
					+ 57.30	
3.	6.7	**7.**	4.782		———	
	+ 8.5		+ 0.308			
	———		———		———	
4.	12.9	**8.**	5.6			
	+ 5.0		0.9			
	———		+ 3.2			
			———			

Set down the following vertically and then add them up:

11. 3.9 + 2.5 + 3.4   **16.** 0.7 + 13.05 + 0.009

12. 6.57 + 31.8 + 5.39   **17.** 6.17 + 15.7 + 28

13. 0.8 + 36.57 + 0.006   **18.** 34.21 + 12 + 2.817

14. 27 + 2.57 + 15.9   **19.** 0.297 + 5.6 + 23.2

15. 28.75 + 6.738   **20.** 0.06 + 7.9 + 4.325

2. Subtraction of decimals

Examples Set down the following vertically and then subtract:
(a) 16.7 − 9.84   (b) 26 − 6.82

Solutions (a) 16.70 − 9.84   16.70
                    = 16.70 − 9.84   − 9.84
                    = 6.86   ———
                                        06.86

(b) 26 − 6.82   26.00
      = 26.00 − 6.82   − 6.82
      = 19.18   ———
                         19.18

Note that 26 is written so that it now has the same number of places after the decimal point as 6.82.

Exercise 6 Copy the following and work them out:

1.	8.4 − 2.1	**5.**	2.54 − 0.09	**9.**	24.00 − 6.58
2.	9.3 − 6.0	**6.**	8.36 − 0.57	**10.**	5.641 − 0.973
3.	8.6 − 2.8	**7.**	15.48 − 7.72		
4.	0.82 − 0.27	**8.**	6.401 − 2.050		

Set down the following vertically and then subtract:

11. $7.6 - 2.1$

12. $23.8 - 6.5$

13. $8.0 - 2.9$

14. $6.4 - 0.64$

15. $21 - 3.8$

16. $8.3 - 0.071$

17. $18 - 0.83$

18. $7.305 - 0.768$

19. $18.2 - 16.42$

20. $35 - 15.7$

F. Multiplication of decimals

Multiplication by 10, 100 and 1000:

To multiply by 10 the figures move one place to the left of the decimal point.

Example (1) $0.46 \times 10 = 4.6$

To multiply by 100 the figures move two places to the left of the decimal point.

Example (2) $6.57 \times 100 = 657.0$ or 657

To multiply by 1000 the figures move three places to the left of the decimal point.

Example (3) $0.45 \times 1000 = 0450.0$ or 450

In Example (3), a zero is added to 45 to make the third place.

Another way of saying all this is that the *decimal point* can be moved one place to the *right* for every zero. Where there are not enough figures, add a zero.

Exercise 7   Find:

1.	0.7×10	**11.**	0.086×1000	**21.**	4.28×100
2.	0.85×10	**12.**	0.754×1000	**22.**	3.2×1000
3.	4.623×100	**13.**	0.07×1000	**23.**	2.61×1000
4.	8.025×100	**14.**	0.63×1000	**24.**	9.32×10
5.	19.07×10	**15.**	1.542×10	**25.**	5.8×100
6.	21.8×10	**16.**	9.28×100	**26.**	2.075×10
7.	0.391×100	**17.**	7.46×100	**27.**	6.839×10
8.	0.471×100	**18.**	2.34×1000	**28.**	6.8×1000
9.	0.6×10	**19.**	8.1×10	**29.**	28.9×1000
10.	0.47×10	**20.**	7.2×100	**30.**	478.5×1000

Examples   (a) 3.6×4 (b) 2.76×7

(c) 3.48×0.6 (d) 0.574×0.07

Solutions   (a)

$$\begin{array}{r} 3.6 \ (1 \text{ d.p.}) \\ \times\, 4 \phantom{(1 \text{ d.p.})} \\ \hline 14.4 \ (1 \text{ d.p.}) \end{array}$$

3.6 has one figure after the decimal point; therefore the answer must also have one figure after the decimal point.

(b)

$$\begin{array}{r} 2.67 \ (2 \text{ d.p.}) \\ \times\, 7 \phantom{(2 \text{ d.p.})} \\ \hline 18.69 \ (2 \text{ d.p.}) \end{array}$$

2.67 has two figures after the decimal point; therefore the answer must also have two figures after the decimal point.

(c)

$$\begin{array}{r} 3.48 \ (2 \text{ d.p.}) \\ \times\, 0.6 \ (1 \text{ d.p.}) \\ \hline 2.088 \ (3 \text{ d.p.}) \end{array}$$

The total number of decimal places after the two numbers 3.48 and 0.6 is 3; therefore the answer must also have 3 places after the decimal point.

(d)

0.574	(3 d.p.)
× 0.07	(2 d.p.)
.04018	(5 d.p.)

The total number of decimal places after the two numbers 0.574 and 0.07 is 5; therefore the answer must also have 5 places after the decimal point. But the answer only has 4 figures, so a zero is placed in front of the 4 to give the fifth place.

Exercise 8   Find:

1.	7.3×3	**11.**	8.4×1.2	**21.**	47×0.5
2.	2.15×4	**12.**	0.76×0.5	**22.**	0.16×0.06
3.	36.4×6	**13.**	3.47×0.7	**23.**	6.09×0.12
4.	5.83×7	**14.**	0.296×0.02	**24.**	5.70×1.1
5.	0.295×4	**15.**	0.378×0.06	**25.**	0.09×0.09
6.	0.178×6	**16.**	4.13×0.04	**26.**	35×0.6
7.	1.92×0.7	**17.**	0.147×0.5	**27.**	0.37×0.08
8.	2.89×0.3	**18.**	0.723×0.07	**28.**	12.63×1.2
9.	7.06×0.8	**19.**	2.5×1.1	**29.**	13.02×0.11
10.	8.03×0.6	**20.**	10.08×9	**30.**	0.07×0.07

G. Division of decimals

1.   Division by a whole number

Before dividing, set down decimal point under decimal point.

Example (1) $5.6 \div 4$
  $= 1.4$

$$4 \, | \, 5.\overset{1}{6}$$
$$\overline{1.4}$$

Example (2) $3.84 \div 6$
  $= 0.64$

$$6 \, | \, 3.8\overset{2}{4}$$
$$\overline{0.64}$$

Example (3) $0.45 \div 9$ $9\overline{)0.\overset{4}{4}5}$ Note that each figure after the
            $= 0.05$ $\overline{0.05}$ decimal is divided and the zero
                                      before the 5 must not be omitted.

Example (4) $7.2 \div 5$ $5\overline{)7.\overset{2}{2}\overset{2}{0}}$ Note that a zero is added to 7.2
            $= 1.44$ $\overline{1.44}$ so that the answer can be worked
                                      out exactly.

Exercise 9 Find:

1. $4.6 \div 2$	**11.** $1.92 \div 2$	**21.** $6.3 \div 9$
2. $8.4 \div 4$	**12.** $3.65 \div 5$	**22.** $1.4 \div 5$
3. $0.96 \div 3$	**13.** $32.5 \div 5$	**23.** $0.8 \div 5$
4. $6.4 \div 4$	**14.** $21.6 \div 8$	**24.** $0.9 \div 4$
5. $5.6 \div 2$	**15.** $0.036 \div 3$	**25.** $0.53 \div 2$
6. $7.2 \div 6$	**16.** $0.45 \div 5$	**26.** $0.372 \div 6$
7. $0.84 \div 7$	**17.** $0.136 \div 4$	**27.** $2.8 \div 8$
8. $9.6 \div 8$	**18.** $19.60 \div 8$	**28.** $2.88 \div 12$
9. $0.65 \div 5$	**19.** $23.73 \div 7$	**29.** $7.7 \div 11$
10. $0.84 \div 6$	**20.** $815.2 \div 4$	**30.** $3.825 \div 9$

2.   **Dividing by 10, 100 and 1000**

To divide by 10 the figures move one place to the right:

Examples (1) (a) $4.6 \div 10 = 0.46$ (b) $0.7 \div 10 = 0.07$
(c) $8 \div 10 = 0.8$

To divide by 100 the figures move two places to the right:

Examples (2) (d) $6.57 \div 100 = 0.0657$ (e) $0.71 \div 100 = 0.0071$

To divide by 1000 the figures move three places to the right:

Examples (3) (f) $23 \div 1000 = 0.023$ (g) $15.1 \div 1000 = 0.0151$

Or, in other words, move the *decimal point* one place to the *left* for each zero.

Exercise 10 Find:

1.	$3.5 \div 10$	**11.**	$0.5 \div 10$	**21.**	$198 \div 100$
2.	$70.6 \div 10$	**12.**	$187 \div 100$	**22.**	$0.68 \div 10$
3.	$28 \div 10$	**13.**	$0.9 \div 100$	**23.**	$62.4 \div 1000$
4.	$251 \div 100$	**14.**	$1.68 \div 100$	**24.**	$3156 \div 1000$
5.	$4.7 \div 100$	**15.**	$3.27 \div 100$	**25.**	$58.2 \div 100$
6.	$18.8 \div 1000$	**16.**	$0.57 \div 100$	**26.**	$17 \div 10$
7.	$0.75 \div 1000$	**17.**	$873 \div 1000$	**27.**	$37.6 \div 10$
8.	$683 \div 10$	**18.**	$0.35 \div 10$	**28.**	$4.327 \div 1000$
9.	$25.6 \div 100$	**19.**	$39 \div 100$	**29.**	$38.78 \div 1000$
10.	$7426 \div 1000$	**20.**	$2.6 \div 10$	**30.**	$4 \div 10$

3. Dividing a decimal by a decimal

Example (1) $6.48 \div 0.4$

$= 64.8 \div 4$ $4 | \overset{2}{6}4.8$

$= 16.2$ $\overline{16.2}$

Before dividing, the divisor (0.4) is first changed to a whole number by multiplying it by 10. Thus the number to be divided (6.48) has also to be multiplied by 10.

Example (2) $0.93 \div 0.03$

$= 093 \div 003$ $3 | 93$

$= 31$ $\overline{31}$

Both divisor and number to be divided are first multiplied by 100.

Example (3) $52 \div 0.5$

$= 520 \div 5$ $5 | 5\overset{2}{2}0$

$= 104$ $\overline{104}$

Both divisor and number to be divided are first multiplied by 10.

Exercise 11 Find:

1.	4.46 ÷ 0.2	**21.**	6.45 ÷ 0.03
2.	6.39 ÷ 0.3	**22.**	8.52 ÷ 0.04
3.	4.48 ÷ 0.4	**23.**	7.38 ÷ 0.06
4.	5.72 ÷ 0.2	**24.**	1.92 ÷ 0.12
5.	7.38 ÷ 0.3	**25.**	3.85 ÷ 0.11
6.	6.15 ÷ 0.5	**26.**	4.2 ÷ 0.05
7.	0.45 ÷ 0.9	**27.**	3.6 ÷ 0.06
8.	0.63 ÷ 0.7	**28.**	7.2 ÷ 1.2
9.	0.125 ÷ 0.5	**29.**	0.3 ÷ 0.4
10.	0.424 ÷ 0.8	**30.**	0.64 ÷ 0.8
11.	0.678 ÷ 0.6	**31.**	2.99 ÷ 1.3
12.	0.315 ÷ 0.05	**32.**	6.02 ÷ 1.4
13.	1.421 ÷ 0.07	**33.**	22.5 ÷ 1.5
14.	2.784 ÷ 0.08	**34.**	0.462 ÷ 2.1
15.	3.020 ÷ 0.05	**35.**	46.5 ÷ 3.1
16.	2.925 ÷ 0.09	**36.**	10.66 ÷ 4.1
17.	7.329 ÷ 0.07	**37.**	62.5 ÷ 0.25
18.	0.1624 ÷ 0.4	**38.**	0.7125 ÷ 0.25
19.	0.738 ÷ 0.03	**39.**	0.918 ÷ 2.7
20.	0.276 ÷ 0.06	**40.**	0.544 ÷ 3.2

H. Ordering decimals

To *order* decimals means to arrange the decimals in order of size, either beginning with the smallest first or beginning with the largest first.

Example (1) Arrange in order of size, smallest first:

0.9,   0.3,   0.7,   0.4

Solution 0.3,   0.4,   0.7,   0.9 (All of the decimals are tenths.)

Example (2) Arrange in order of size, smallest first:

0.5, 0.003, 0.02, 0.15

Solution The decimals are not all of the same name.

0.003 has the greatest number of figures after the decimal point.

That is, three figures.

Add zeros to the right of the other numbers so that they too have three figures after the decimal points.

Thus   0.5,   0.003, 0.02,   0.15

become 0.500, 0.003, 0.020, 0.150

These in order are: 0.003,   0.020,   0.150,   0.500

that is: 0.003,   0.02,   0.15,   0.5

Exercise 12 Arrange the decimals in each question in order of size, smallest first:

1. 0.2, 0.7, 0.6, 0.1

2. 0.5, 0.8, 0.3, 0.9

3. 0.38, 0.19, 0.57, 0.13

4. 0.75, 0.56, 0.49, 0.63

5. 0.41, 0.5, 0.4, 0.38

6. 0.6, 0.12, 0.3, 0.25

7. 0.08, 0.017, 0.011, 0.68

8. 0.013, 0.05, 0.25, 0.005

9. 0.002, 0.04, 0.3, 0.14

10. 0.125, 0.2, 0.14, 0.8

Chapter Nine

Percentages

A. Changing fractions to percentages

Remember: The short form for percentage is 'per cent'.
The sign for per cent is %,
Per cent means 'out of 100'.

$$15\% = 15 \text{ out of } 100$$
$$= \frac{15}{100}$$
$$8\% = \frac{8}{100}$$

To change a fraction to a percentage, multiply it by 100%.

Examples   Change the following fractions to percentages:

(a) $\dfrac{7}{10}$

(b) $\dfrac{1}{4}$

(c) $\dfrac{16}{40}$

Solutions   (a) $\dfrac{7}{10} = 70\%$ $\dfrac{7}{\cancel{10}_{1}} \times \dfrac{\cancel{100}^{10}\%}{1} = 70\%$

(b) $\dfrac{1}{4} = 25\%$ $\dfrac{1}{\cancel{4}_{1}} \times \dfrac{\cancel{100}^{25}\%}{1} = 25\%$

(c) $\dfrac{16}{40} = 40\%$ $\dfrac{\cancel{16}^{4}}{\cancel{40}_{\cancel{10}_{1}}} \times \dfrac{\cancel{100}^{10}\%}{1} = 40\%$

Exercise 1 Change the following fractions to percentages:

1. $\frac{6}{10}$	**7.** $\frac{8}{20}$	**13.** $\frac{17}{25}$	**19.** $\frac{18}{100}$	**25.** $\frac{12}{15}$
2. $\frac{9}{10}$	**8.** $\frac{7}{20}$	**14.** $\frac{14}{50}$	**20.** $\frac{76}{100}$	**26.** $\frac{18}{45}$
3. $\frac{4}{10}$	**9.** $\frac{10}{20}$	**15.** $\frac{26}{50}$	**21.** $\frac{27}{100}$	**27.** $\frac{3}{4}$
4. $\frac{5}{10}$	**10.** $\frac{17}{20}$	**16.** $\frac{35}{50}$	**22.** $\frac{18}{40}$	**28.** $\frac{1}{4}$
5. $\frac{3}{10}$	**11.** $\frac{9}{25}$	**17.** $\frac{3}{5}$	**23.** $\frac{8}{40}$	**29.** $\frac{80}{200}$
6. $\frac{15}{20}$	**12.** $\frac{13}{25}$	**18.** $\frac{4}{5}$	**24.** $\frac{30}{60}$	**30.** $\frac{60}{300}$

B. Changing percentages to fractions in their lowest terms

Examples Change: **(a)** 60% **(b)** 45% to fractions in their lowest terms.

Solutions **(a)** $60\% = \frac{2}{5}$ $60\% = \frac{\overset{3}{\cancel{60}}}{\underset{5}{\cancel{100}}} = \frac{3}{5}$ (Cancel by 20)

(b) $45\% = \frac{9}{20}$ $45\% = \frac{\overset{9}{\cancel{45}}}{\underset{20}{\cancel{100}}} = \frac{9}{20}$ (Cancel by 5)

Exercise 2 Change the following percentages to fractions in their lowest terms:

1. 30%	**6.** 90%	**11.** 55%	**16.** 85%
2. 10%	**7.** 50%	**12.** 14%	**17.** 72%
3. 40%	**8.** 25%	**13.** 8%	**18.** 24%
4. 70%	**9.** 75%	**14.** 65%	**19.** 38%
5. 80%	**10.** 35%	**15.** 5%	**20.** 84%

C. Finding a percentage of a number, money, mass, length, etc.

Examples   Find: **(a)**   10% of $300   **(b)**   25% of 80

(c)   10% of $25.50

Solutions   **(a)**   10% of $300 $= \$30$ $\dfrac{\overset{1}{\cancel{10}}}{\underset{\underset{1}{\cancel{10}}}{\cancel{100}}} \times \dfrac{\overset{30}{\cancel{\$300}}}{1} = \$30$

(b)   25% of 80 $= 20$ $\dfrac{\overset{1}{\cancel{25}}}{\underset{\underset{1}{\diagup}}{\cancel{100}}} \times \dfrac{\overset{20}{\cancel{80}}}{1} = 20$

(c)   10% of $25.50 $= \$2.55$ $\dfrac{\overset{1}{\cancel{10}}}{\underset{\underset{1}{\cancel{10}}}{\cancel{100}}} \times \dfrac{\overset{2.55}{\cancel{\$25.50}}}{1} = \$2.55$

$or \quad \dfrac{10}{100} \times \$25.50 = \dfrac{\overset{1}{\cancel{10}}}{\underset{\underset{1}{\cancel{10}}}{\cancel{100}}} \times \dfrac{\overset{255}{\cancel{2550}\cancel{c}}}{1}$

$= 255 \, ¢$

$= \$2.55$

Exercise 3   Find:

1. 10% of $100	**11.**	20% of 60
2. 10% of $400	**12.**	5% of 100
3. 10% of $500	**13.**	16% of 75
4. 10% of $800	**14.**	100% of 300 m
5. 10% of $700	**15.**	4% of 900 g
6. 25% of $200	**16.**	5% of 1600 marbles
7. 25% of $600	**17.**	5% of 900 apples
8. 25% of 300	**18.**	20% of 700 eggs
9. 25% of 900	**19.**	15% of 1000 pupils
10. 25% of 1000	**20.**	8% of 300 coconuts

21.	25% of 40 L		**26.**	60% of 40 km
22.	100% of $7000		**27.**	15% of 100 kg
23.	50% of $1700		**28.**	75% of 200 cm
24.	10% of $46.60		**29.**	40% of 40 m
25.	10% of $15.20		**30.**	50% of 400 m

D. Problems involving percentages

Example (1) There are 40 pupils in a class. 60 per cent of them are girls. How many are **(a)** girls **(b)** boys?

Solution **(a)** No. of girls $= 60\%$ of 40 $\dfrac{\overset{3}{\cancel{60}}}{\underset{\cancel{5}{}_{1}}{\cancel{100}}} \times \dfrac{\overset{8}{\cancel{40}}}{1} = 24$

(b) No. of boys $= 40 - 24 = 16$

Example (2) Ann had $200. She spent 25% of it at the supermarket. How much had she left?

First Solution   Ann spent 25%
Ann had $100\% - 25\% = 75\%$ left

$\therefore$ Amount of money left $= 75\%$ of $200 $\dfrac{75}{\underset{1}{\cancel{100}}} \times \$\overset{2}{\cancel{200}}$
$= \$150$
$= \$150$

Second Solution   Ann spent 25% of $200 $\dfrac{25}{\underset{1}{\cancel{100}}} \times \dfrac{\$\overset{2}{\cancel{200}}}{1} = \$50$
$= \$50$
Amount left $= \$200 - \$50$
$= \$150$

Exercise 4

1. There are 800 pupils at a certain school. 45% of them are girls.
  (a) How many girls are at the school?
  (b) How many boys are at the school?

2. Mother had a box which contained 90 eggs. 10% of them were bad.

(a) How many eggs were good?

(b) How many eggs were bad?

3. Mr Richards the farmer had 200 chickens. 25% of them died.

(a) How many chickens died?

(b) How many chickens remained alive?

4. Mary's mother gave her $20 for pocket money. She spent 10% of it.

(a) How much did she spend?

(b) How much had she left?

5. A shopkeeper bought 300 buns. She sold 80% of them.

(a) How many did she sell?

(b) How many had she left?

6. Peter had 100 marbles. He gave 35% of them to Sam, and the rest to Pedro. How many did he give to Pedro?

7. My teacher gave us 80 problems in mathematics to do. I got 90% of them correct. How many problems did I get wrong?

8. In a mathematics test Andy got 18 marks out of 25. What percentage is this?

9. Our school bus was carrying 120 pupils. If 15% of them were standing, how many were sitting?

10. Which is greater and by how much:

(a)   10% of $500 or   (b)   8% of $600?

E. Profit and loss

1. Profit and loss, percentage profit and loss

Profit and loss are two terms which concern business people and business places. These businesses could be big or small. The following are some who are involved with profit and loss: Snowcone vendors, nutsellers, canteens, village shops, hotels, department stores and garment factories.

In this section we are only concerned with the profit and loss involved with buying and selling.

If the Selling Price (S.P.) is greater than the Cost Price (C.P.) there is a *profit*.

If the S.P. is less than the C.P., there is a *loss*.

Profit $=$ S.P. $-$ C.P.

Loss $=$ C.P. $-$ S.P.

Both the profit and the loss can be expressed as a percentage of the cost price:

Profit as a percentage $= \dfrac{\text{Profit}}{\text{C.P.}} \times 100\%$

Loss as a percentage $= \dfrac{\text{Loss}}{\text{C.P.}} \times 100\%$

Examples (1) An article that cost $20 was sold for $25.

Find: **(a)** the profit   **(b)** the percentage profit.

Solutions   **(a)** Profit $=$ S.P. $-$ C.P.

$= \$25 - \$20$

$= \$5$

(b) Profit % $= \dfrac{\text{Profit}}{\text{C.P.}} \times 100\%$

$= \dfrac{\$5}{\$25} \times \dfrac{100\%}{1}$

$= 5 \times 4\%$

$= 20\%$

Examples (2) An article that cost $25 was sold for $21.

Find: **(a)** the loss   **(b)** the percentage loss.

Solutions   **(a)** Loss $=$ C.P. $-$ S.P.

$= \$25 - \$21$

$= \$4$

(b) % Loss $= \dfrac{\text{Loss}}{\text{C.P.}} \times 100\%$

$= \dfrac{\$4}{\$25} \times \overset{4}{\cancel{100}}\%$

$= 4 \times 4\%$

$= 16\%$

Exercise 5 Complete the following table:

	C.P.	S.P.	Profit	Profit %
1.	$10	$12	. . .	. . .
2.	$20	$24	. . .	. . .
3.	$30	$60	. . .	. . .
4.	$40	$50	. . .	. . .
5.	$100	$112	. . .	. . .

Complete the following table:

	C.P.	S.P.	Loss	Loss %
6.	$15	$12	. . .	. . .
7.	$25	$20	. . .	. . .
8.	$50	$36	. . .	. . .
9.	$80	$64	. . .	. . .
10.	$100	$92	. . .	. . .

Complete the following table:

	C.P.	S.P.	Profit	Loss	Profit %	Loss %
11.	$5	$4	. . .	. . .	. . .	. . .
12.	$12	$15	. . .	. . .	. . .	. . .
13.	$25	$50	. . .	. . .	. . .	. . .
14.	$35	$49	. . .	. . .	. . .	. . .
15.	$60	$45	. . .	. . .	. . .	. . .
16.	$100	$25	. . .	. . .	. . .	. . .
17.	$300	$360	. . .	. . .	. . .	. . .
18.	$2.50	$3.00	. . .	. . .	. . .	. . .
19.	$400	$240	. . .	. . .	. . .	. . .
20.	$500	$600	. . .	. . .	. . .	. . .

21. A man bought an article for $125 and sold it for $110. Calculate his loss.

22. A shopkeeper bought 300 cakes for $60.00. He sold the cakes at 30¢ each. What was his profit?

23. An article was bought for $40 and sold for $30. Calculate
(a) the loss (b) the loss per cent.

24. The school canteen buys each case of 24 soft drinks for
$12.00. If it sells a soft drink for 60¢, what is the profit
on one case of soft drinks?

25. A TV dealer bought a TV for $300 and sold it for $480.
Calculate his percentage profit.

2. Finding the selling price

Example (1) An article was bought for $20 and sold at a profit of 10%. How
much was it sold for?

Solution

C.P. = $20

Profit = 10% of $20

= $2

S.P. = C.P. + Profit

= $20 + $2

= $22

$$10\% \text{ of } \$20 = \frac{10}{100} \times \frac{\$20}{1}$$
$$= \$2$$

Example (2) A man bought an article for $60 and sold it at a loss of 15%.
How much did he sell it for?

Solution

C.P. = $60

Loss = 15% of $60

= $9

S.P. = C.P. − Loss

= $60 − $9

= $51

$$15\% \text{ of } \$60 = \frac{15}{100} \times \frac{\$60}{1}$$
$$= \$9$$

Exercise 6 Complete the following table:

	C.P.	Profit %	S.P.
1.	$10	10%	. . .
2.	$15	20%	. . .
3.	$60	5%	. . .
4.	$150	8%	. . .
5.	$200	10%	. . .

Complete the following table:

	C.P.	Loss %	S.P.
6.	$12	25%	. . .
7.	$80	15%	. . .
8.	$100	12%	. . .
9.	$250	20%	. . .
10.	$400	5%	. . .

Complete the following table:

	C.P.	Profit %	Loss %	S.P.
11.	$4	75%		. . .
12.	$15	100%		. . .
13.	$20		50%	. . .
14.	$40	10%		. . .
15.	$50		5%	. . .
16.	$100	12%		. . .
17.	$4.50		10%	. . .
18.	$600		25%	. . .

19. An article was bought for $50 and sold at a profit of 10%. How much was it sold for?

20. A man bought a record player for $160 and sold it at a loss of 15%. How much did he sell it for?

F. Discount

Discount is the reduction in price of an article. For example, if a shirt is priced at $19.95 and a discount of $5.00 is given for buying the shirt for cash, then the shirt is reduced by $5.00 and the customer pays $19.95 − $5.00 = $14.95 for the shirt.

Discount is usually given when a customer pays cash, or pays within a certain time limit. It is often expressed as a percentage of the selling price.

Example (1) At a sale, a bicycle which usually costs $450 was reduced by $75. How much did a customer pay for it?

Solution	Price of bicycle = $450
	Discount = $75
	Customer paid $450 − $75 = $375

Example (2) A discount of 10% was given on a TV set which usually costs $800. How much must be paid for this TV set?

Solution   Usual price of TV set = $800 $\frac{10}{100} \times \frac{\$800}{1} = \$80$

Discount 10% of $800 = $80

Customer paid $800 − $80

= $720

Exercise 7 Complete the following table:

	Price of article	Discount	Amount actually paid
1.	$40	$10	. . .
2.	$120	$25	. . .
3.	$100	$15	. . .
4.	$450	$90	. . .
5.	$1225	$122.50	. . .
6.	$50	10%	. . .
7.	$80	15%	. . .
8.	$100	15%	. . .
9.	$180	5%	. . .
10.	$200	8%	. . .
11.	$450	20%	. . .
12.	$800	5%	. . .
13.	$1000	25%	. . .
14.	$1200	40%	. . .
15.	$1250	25%	. . .

16. At the 'back to school' sale, shoes which usually cost $45.50 are reduced by $15.75. How much must be paid for them?

17. A radio is priced at $460, subject to a 15% discount for cash. How much did a customer pay for the radio if he paid cash?

18. At a sale a living room suite which costs $1600 was reduced by 25%. How much must be paid for this suite?

19. How much must be paid for a damaged stove which costs $750 and is reduced by 40%?

20. A customer is offered a 10% discount if he pays in 3 months for a colour TV set which costs $1125. How much does a customer pay for the TV set if he accepts this offer?

G. Miscellaneous problems

Exercise 8   Complete:

1. $\dfrac{7}{20} = \ldots\%$ **3.** $80\% = \dfrac{}{100}$

2. $35\% = \dfrac{7}{}$ **4.** $64\% = \dfrac{}{25}$

5. What is 20% of $60.00?

6. Express 16 as a percentage of 40.

7. A farmer planted 40% of his land with carrots, 35% with sweet potatoes and the rest with onions. What percentage did he plant with onions?

8. A customer had to pay 8% tax on the value of items that he imported. He paid a total tax of $40.00 for the items. What was the value of the imported items?

9. A vendor bought 200 water coconuts for $90.00 and sold them at $1.00 each. What was his percentage profit?

10. At a sale a toaster oven, which usually costs $200.00, is reduced by 25%. How much does a customer pay for the toaster oven at the reduced price?

Chapter Ten

Angles

Introduction

When one straight line meets another straight line an angle is formed. The two straight lines are called *arms*. See Fig. 1.

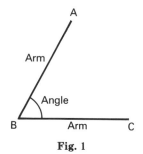

Fig. 1

As the arm AB moves closer to the arm BC, the angle gets smaller. See Fig. 2.

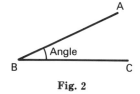

Fig. 2

As the arm AB turns away from BC the angle gets bigger. See Fig. 3.

An angle is therefore the *amount of turn.*

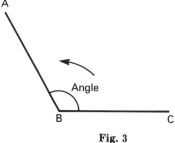

Fig. 3

A. Right angles

When AB is perpendicular to BC, the angle formed is called a *right angle.* See Fig. 4.

A right angle measures 90 degrees (90°).

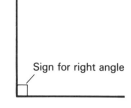

Sign for right angle

Fig. 4

The four corners of your exercise book are all right angles.

Find other examples of right angles in the classroom. Use two straight edges to form right angles in different positions. Draw right angles in different positions from the one represented in Fig. 4.

The diagram to the right contains 40 different right angles. Try to find them.

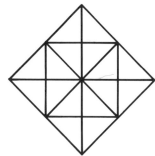

B. Acute angles

All angles that measure less than a right angle are called *acute angles.* See Fig. 5.

So an angle that measures 65°, for example, is an acute angle.

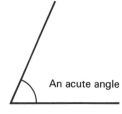

An acute angle

Fig. 5

Name other measurements that are acute angles.

Use two straight edges to form acute angles.

Draw acute angles in different positions from the one represented in Fig. 5.

C. Straight angles

If AB in Fig. 6 moves so that it now makes ABC a straight line, the angle formed is called a *straight angle*. A straight angle measures 180°. See Fig. 7.

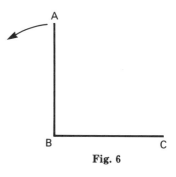

Fig. 6

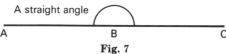

A straight angle

Fig. 7

Draw straight angles in different positions from the one represented in Fig. 7.

D. Obtuse angles

All angles that measure more than 90° but less than 180° are called *obtuse angles*. See Fig. 8.

An angle that measures 126° is an obtuse angle.

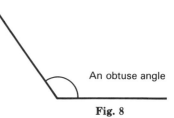

An obtuse angle

Fig. 8

Name other measurements that are obtuse angles.

Use two straight edges to form obtuse angles.

Draw obtuse angles in different positions from the one represented in Fig. 8.

E. Reflex angles

If AB in Fig. 9 moves so that the angle formed is now more than a straight angle (2 right angles) but less than 4 right angles, the angle is called a *reflex angle*. See Fig. 10.

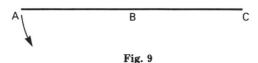

Fig. 9

Note that the angle on the inside in Fig. 10 is an obtuse angle.

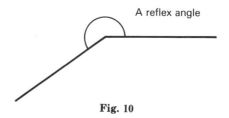

Fig. 10

All angles that measure between 180° and 360° are called reflex angles. So an angle that measures 196° is a reflex angle.

Name other measurements that are reflex angles.

Use two straight lines to form reflex angles.

Draw reflex angles in different positions from the one represented in Fig. 10.

F. The circle

When AB in Fig. 11 moves so that it fits exactly on BC, it has now traced out a circle. In a circle there are 4 right angles, or 360°. See Fig. 12.

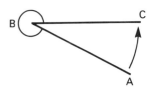

Fig. 11

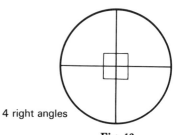

4 right angles

Fig. 12

Summary

1. A right angle measures 90°.

2. An acute angle measures less than 90°.

3. A straight angle measures 180°.

4. An obtuse angle measures more than 90° but less than 180°.

5. A reflex angle measures more than 180° but less than 360°.

6. In a circle there are 4 right angles or 360°.

Note: The clock face can be used to demonstrate the amount of turn for all these angles.

Exercise 1 **1.** Draw a diagram to represent each of the following angles. Then using names from here (acute, obtuse, right, straight, reflex) write the name of each angle underneath it.

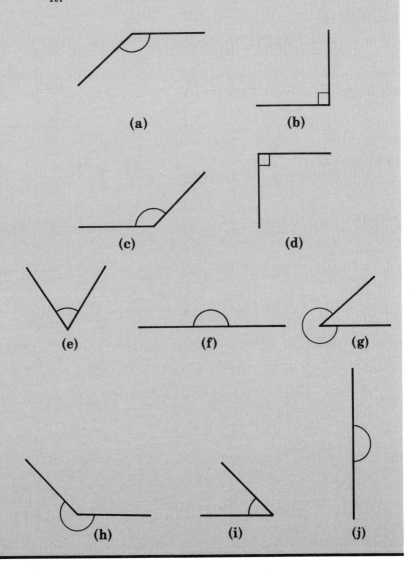

(a)

(b)

(c)

(d)

(e)

(f)

(g)

(h)

(i)

(j)

2. Complete the following table (the first one has been done for you):

Angle	76°	89°	109°	180°	264°	90°	31°	288°	178°
Kind	acute								

G. Calculations based on the right angle

If a right angle is divided into two or more angles the sum of the smaller angles must add to 90°.

Example (1) The angles marked *a* in the diagram to the right are equal. Find the value of *a*.

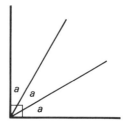

Solution $a = 90° \div 3 = 30°$

Example (2) Find the value of *x* in the diagram to the right.

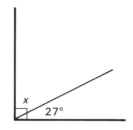

Solution $x = 90° - 27° = 63°$

Exercise 2 **1.** Find the value of each angle marked with a letter:

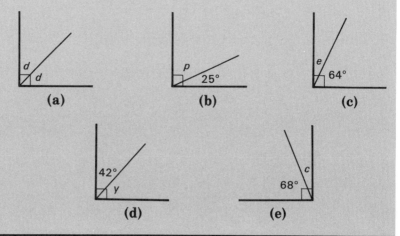

(a) (b) (c)

(d) (e)

H. Calculations based on the straight angle

If a straight angle is divided into two or more angles, the sum of the angles must add to 180°.

Example (1) Find the value of c in the diagram to the right.

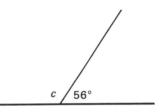

Solution $c = 180° - 56° = 124°$

Example (2) The angles marked b in the diagram to the right are equal. Find the value of b.

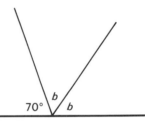

Solution $b + b = 180° - 70° = 110°$

$b = 110° \div 2 = 55°$

Check: $55° + 55° + 70° = 180°$

Exercise 3 **1.** Find the value of each angle marked with a letter:

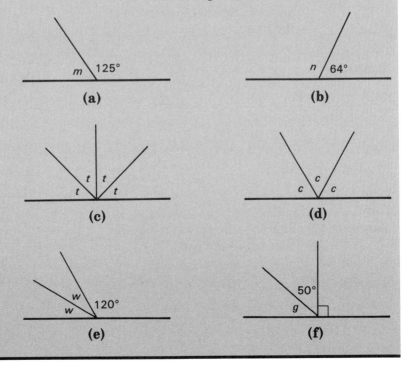

(a)

(b)

(c)

(d)

(e)

(f)

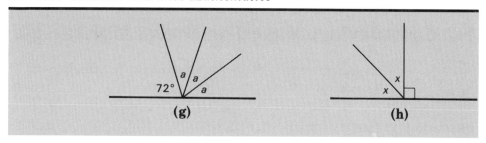

(g)   (h)

I. Calculations based on the circle

If a circle is divided into a number of angles, the sum of the angles must add to 360°.

Example (1) Find the value of x in the diagram to the right.

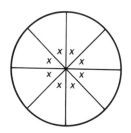

Solution $x = 360° ÷ 8$

           $= 45°$

Example (2) Find the value of each unknown marked angle in the diagram to the right.

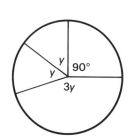

Solution

$$y + y + 3y = 360° - 90°$$
$$= 270°$$
$$\therefore \quad 5y = 270°$$
$$y = 270° ÷ 5$$
$$= 54°$$
$$3y = 54° \times 3$$
$$= 162°$$

Example (3) Find the value of f and h in the diagram to the right.

Solution $f = 180° ÷ 4 = 45°$

           $h = 180° ÷ 3 = 60°$

Exercise 4 **1.** Find the value of the unknown marked angles:

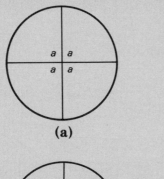

(a)

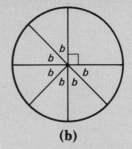

(b)

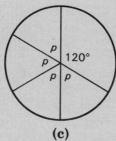

(c)

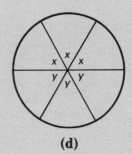

(d)

Exercise 5 Find the value of each unknown marked angle in each diagram:

1.

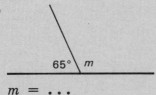

$m = \ldots$

4.

$a = \ldots$

2.

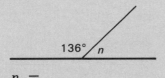

$n = \ldots$

5.

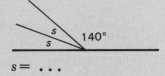

$s = \ldots$

3.

$p = \ldots$

6.

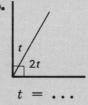

$t = \ldots$

$2t = \ldots$

7.

$v = \ldots$

9.

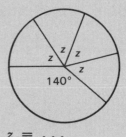

$z = \ldots$

8.

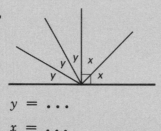

$y = \ldots$

$x = \ldots$

10.

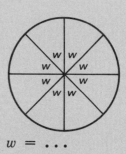

$w = \ldots$

Look at the clock to the right and then answer the questions that follow.

11. What is the size of the angle between 1 and 2?

12. What is the size of the angle between 2 and 5?

13. What is the size of the angle between 6 and 12?

14. Through how many degrees does the hour hand of the clock pass between 3 o'clock and 6 o'clock?

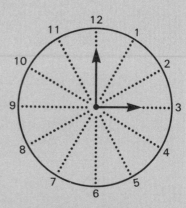

15. Through how many degrees does the hour hand of the clock pass between 7 o'clock and 11 o'clock?

Chapter Eleven

Plane Figures

A. Triangles

A triangle has 3 sides and 3 angles. If 2 sides of a triangle measure the same length, we call it an *isosceles* triangle.

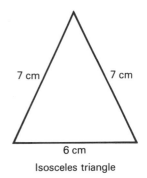

Isosceles triangle

If all 3 sides of a triangle measure the same length, we call it an *equilateral* triangle.

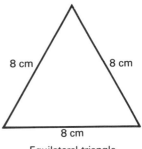

Equilateral triangle

If all 3 sides of a triangle measure different lengths, we call it a *scalene* triangle.

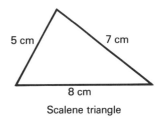

Scalene triangle

The triangle to the right is a scalene triangle, but it is also called a right-angled triangle because one angle is a right angle.

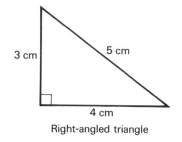

Right-angled triangle

Exercise 1 What kind of triangle (isosceles, equilateral, scalene, right-angled) is each of the following?

1.

7 cm   7 cm

7 cm

2.

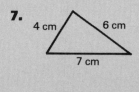

5 cm   9 cm

10 cm

3.

8 cm   10 cm

6 cm

4.

5 cm

7 cm   7 cm

5.

4.5 cm   6 cm

7.5 cm

6.

5.5 cm   5.5 cm

6 cm

7.

4 cm   6 cm

7 cm

8.

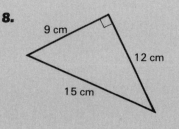

9 cm

12 cm

15 cm

B. The square and the rectangle

The square

1. The 4 angles are equal; each angle measures 90°.

2. The 4 sides are equal.

3. The opposite sides are parallel.

   AB is parallel to DC and AD is parallel to BC.

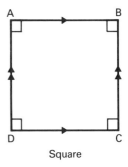
Square

Parallel lines are lines such that, no matter how far you produce them in either direction, they will never meet. For example, the lines in your English exercise book are parallel. Two or more lines can be parallel.

Cut out a square from squared paper. Cut it into triangles like the one in the figure to the right. What do you notice about the size of each triangle?

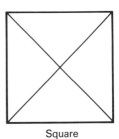
Square

The rectangle

1. The 4 angles are equal; each angle measures 90°.

2. The opposite sides are equal: PQ = SR, PS = QR.

3. The opposite sides are parallel.

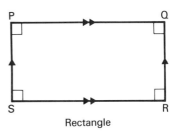
Rectangle

   PQ is parallel to SR and PS is parallel to QR.

Draw a rectangle on squared paper. Divide it into triangles like the one in the figure to the right. What do you notice about the area of opposite triangles?

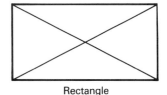
Rectangle

Exercise 2 **1.** What properties of the square are also properties of the rectangle?

2. Which is true or false?

(a) A rectangle is a square.

(b) A square is a rectangle.

3. Draw a square and a rectangle which have the same area.

C. The parallelogram

1. The opposite angles are equal: angle L = angle N, and angle P = angle M.

2. The opposite sides are equal: LM = PN, and LP = MN.

3. The opposite sides are parallel: LP is parallel to MN, and LM is parallel to PN.

Look at the parallelogram on squared paper below. What is its area? Can you find out how to calculate the area of a parallelogram?

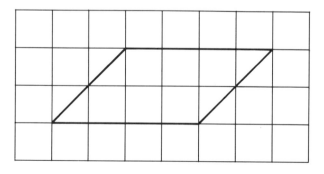

D. The rhombus

1. The opposite angles are equal: angle P = angle R, and angle Q = angle S.

2. The 4 sides are equal.

3. The opposite sides are parallel: PQ is parallel to SR, and PS is parallel to QR.

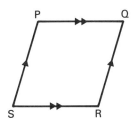

Draw a rhombus on squared paper. Find out the area of it. Divide your rhombus like the one in the figure below.

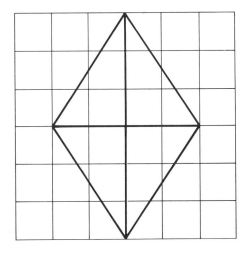

What do you notice about the size of each triangle? Can you find out how to calculate the area of a rhombus?

E. The trapezium

1. The trapezium has 4 sides.

2. It has only one pair of parallel sides: WZ is parallel to XY.

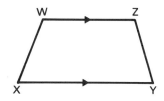

Look at the trapeziums below. What is the area of each one?

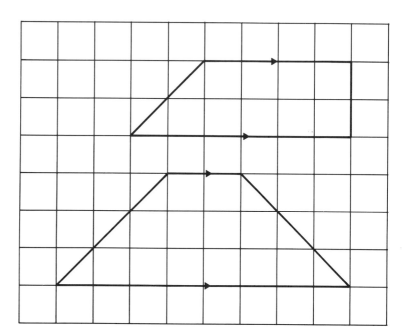

Can you find out how to calculate the area of a trapezium?

F. The circle

Look at Figs. 1 to 3 and learn the names of some of the parts. The line which traces out the circle is called the circumference. The point O is called the *centre* of the circle.

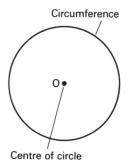

Fig. 1

The line AB in Fig. 2 is called the *diameter*. The diameter divides the circle into 2 equal parts. Each part is called a semicircle. One half of a diameter is called a radius.

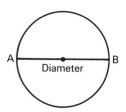

Fig. 2

OB in Fig. 3 is called a *radius* (the plural of radius is radii).

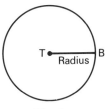

Fig. 3

If diameter $(d) = 10$ cm $\therefore$ radius $(r) = 5$ cm

If radius $(r) = 7$ cm $\therefore$ diameter $(d) = 14$ cm

Exercise 3 Complete the following for any circle:

1. $r = 6$ cm $\therefore$ $d = \ldots$
2. $r = 14$ mm $\therefore$ $d = \ldots$
3. $d = 16$ mm $\therefore$ $r = \ldots$
4. $d = 21$ mm $\therefore$ $r = \ldots$
5. $r = 5.5$ cm $\therefore$ $d = \ldots$
6. $d = 42$ mm $\therefore$ $r = \ldots$

G. Miscellaneous questions

Exercise 4 Study the diagram below, which is drawn accurately, and then answer the questions that follow:

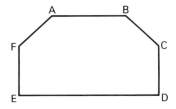

1. Name a line parallel to ED.
2. Name a line equal in length to CD.
3. Name a horizontal line.
4. Name a perpendicular line.
5. How many right angles are there in this figure?

Chapter Twelve

Solid Figures

Introduction

A solid figure is one that takes up space. Some figures that take up space are *irregular* and others are *regular*. Examples of irregular solids are a loaf of bread, an electric iron and a telephone. In this chapter, we want to be able to recognise some regular solids and learn more about their properties.

All regular figures have three dimensions. The dimensions are either in the form of length, width and height, or area of base and height. Remember that area is equivalent to two dimensions. Here are diagrams of the solids that we want to learn about:

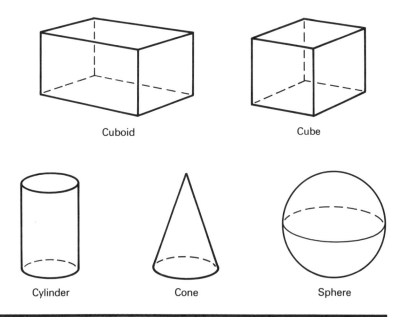

Cuboid	Cube
Cylinder	Cone	Sphere

A. The cuboid

The cuboid looks like a box. Look at the diagrams to the right. Fig. 1 shows the following parts of a cuboid: face, edge and corner.

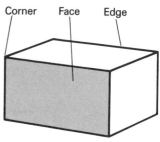

Corner Face Edge

Fig. 1

The broken lines in Fig. 2 show the edges that you cannot see.

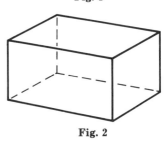

Fig. 2

Collect articles that have the shape of a cuboid and use them to help you complete the table below:

Shape	Number of faces	Number of edges	Number of corners
Cuboid	...	...	...

What shape does each face of a cuboid have?

What do you notice about the opposite faces of each cuboid?

B. The cube

The cube is a special cuboid. A die (the plural is dice) is a good example of a cube.

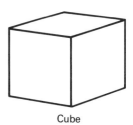

Cube

Cut a cube in two equal halves. What shape does each half make?

Can you halve a cube so that each half will form a different shape from the shape above?

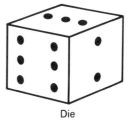

Die

Collect articles that have the shape of a cube and use them to help you complete the table below:

Shape	Number of faces	Number of edges	Number of corners
Cube	. . .	. . .	. . .

What shape does each face of a cube have?

What properties of a cube are also properties of a cuboid?

C. The cylinder

A cylinder has a curved face and two flat faces.

Some cylinders are opened at one or both ends.

An orange-juice tin is a good example of a cylinder.

Cylinder

Collect articles that have the shape of a cylinder and use them to help you complete the table below:

Shape	Number of faces	Number of edges	Number of corners
Cylinder	. . .	. . .	. . .

What shape does the flat face of a cylinder have?

What shape do the edges have?

In what way is a cylinder similar to a cuboid?

For you to do

Take the card on which toilet paper is wrapped (this is a cylinder opened at both ends) and cut it in a straight line along its curved face to form a plane figure.

What shape does the card now have?

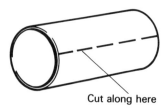
Cut along here

Shapes that have a pair of the same flat faces opposite to one another are called *prisms*.

The diagrams below show a number of prisms.

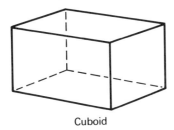

Cuboid

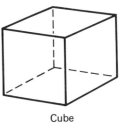

Cube

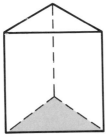

Prism with a triangle
as base

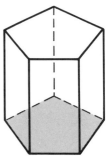

Prism with a
pentagon as base

D. The cone

To make a cone, draw a circle on a piece of paper. Cut out a piece from the circle (see Fig. 1).

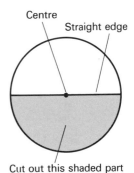

Centre

Straight edge

Cut out this shaded part

Fig. 1

Fold the card remaining to form a cone by putting the two straight edges together and sticking them (see Fig. 2).

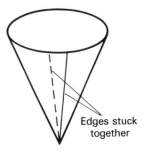

Edges stuck
together

Fig. 2

If the top of a cone is cut off it is called a *truncated cone.*

Truncated cone

Give the names of articles that are truncated cones.

Collect articles having the shape of a cone and use them to help you complete the table below:

Shape	Number of faces	Number of edges	Number of corners
Cone	. . .	. . .	. . .

The cone belongs to a family of solids called *pyramids.*

The diagrams below show a number of pyramids.

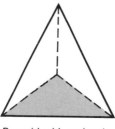

Pyramid with a triangle
as base

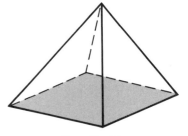

Pyramid with a
square as base

Pyramid with a
circle as base (cone)

E. The sphere

A sphere is easy to recognise.
Any article that has the shape
of a ball is called a *sphere*.

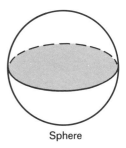

Sphere

Collect articles that have the shape of a sphere and use them to
help you complete the table below:

Shape	Number of faces	Number of edges	Number of corners
Sphere	. . .	. . .	. . .

For you to do

Cut an orange in half. Each half of the orange is called a hemi-
sphere. What shape does each new face have?

Exercise 1   Use a name from the list (cuboid, cone, cylinder, cube, sphere)
which best describes each of the following articles:

1. A football   . . .   **6.** A marble   . . .

2. A stick of chalk . . .   **7.** A garden hose   . . .

3. Your textbook   . . .   **8.** A funnel   . . .

4. A match box   . . .   **9.** A refrigerator   . . .

5. A cigarette   . . .   **10.** An egg   . . .

Exercise 2   **1.** Which shape has only one face?

2. How many faces does a cuboid have?

3. What shape does the flat face of a cylinder have?

4. How many edges does a cylinder have?

5. How many corners does a cone have?

6. If an orange is cut in half, what shape does its new surface
have?

7. Which shape has the same number of faces, edges and
corners as a cuboid?

Write true or false:

8. A cone is a cuboid: . . .

9. A cube is a cuboid: . . .

10. A cuboid has all the properties of a cube: . . .

11. A circle is a solid figure: . . .

Underline the correct words:

12. If the opposite faces of a solid are the same it is called a (prism, pyramid).

13. A cone is an example of a (prism, pyramid).

14. Each face of a cube is (rectangular, square, circular).

15. An orange is an example of a (cone, circle, sphere).

The diagram shows a drinking glass. Look at it carefully and then complete questions 16 to 18.

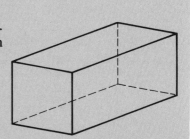

16. The glass has . . . faces.

17. The glass has . . . corners.

18. The glass has . . . edges.

This diagram shows a cuboid. Study in carefully and then answer questions 19 and 20.

19. How many *pairs* of parallel edges does the cuboid have?

20. How many right angles are in this cuboid?

Chapter Thirteen

Lines of Symmetry

If a sheet of paper is folded into two equal parts so that one part exactly covers the other part, then the folded line is called a *line of symmetry.*

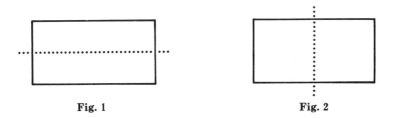

Fig. 1   Fig. 2

Figs. 1 and 2 show the same sheet of paper folded in two different ways along the dotted lines. Each dotted line is called a line of symmetry.

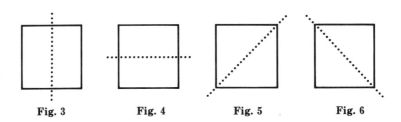

Fig. 3   Fig. 4   Fig. 5   Fig. 6

Figs. 3 to 6 above show a square sheet of paper folded in 4 different ways along the dotted lines. Each dotted line is a line of symmetry.

Look at the figure to the right.

Question: Is the dotted line a line of symmetry?

Answer: Yes.

Why? When folded along the dotted line the plain part will cover exactly the shaded part.

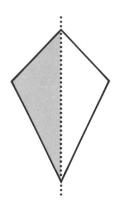

Look again at the same figure folded differently.

Question: Is the dotted line a line of symmetry?

Answer: No.

Why? When folded along the dotted line the plain part will not cover exactly the shaded part.

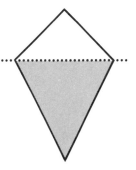

Exercise 1   In which diagrams is the dotted line a line of symmetry?

1.

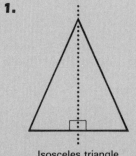

Isosceles triangle

3.

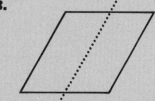

Rhombus

2.

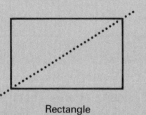

Rectangle

4.

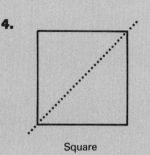

Square

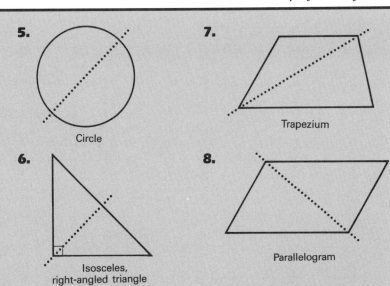

5. Circle

6. Isosceles, right-angled triangle

7. Trapezium

8. Parallelogram

Exercise 2 Draw the following figures on squared paper and complete them so that the line AB becomes a line of symmetry.

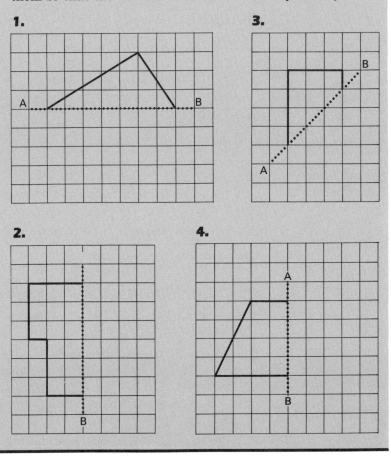

1.

2.

3.

4.

5.

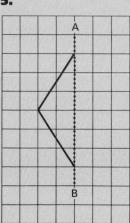

7.

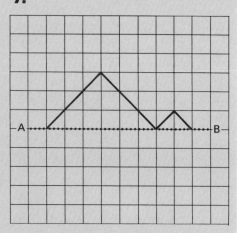

6.

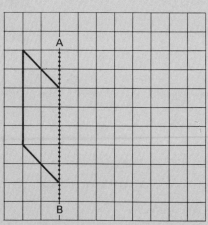

8.

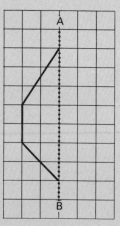

Exercise 3 **1.** Draw the following figures on squared paper:

(a) square   (b) rectangle   (c) rhombus
(d) equilateral triangle   (e) semicircle

2. Draw in all the lines of symmetry for each of the figures.

Here is an example:

This figure has two lines of symmetry.

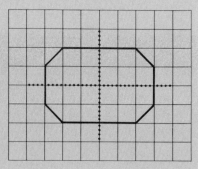

Exercise 4 How many lines of symmetry does each of the figures below have? Some figures may have none.

1.

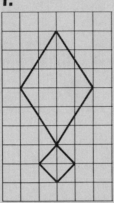

5.

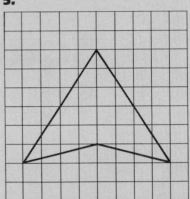

2.

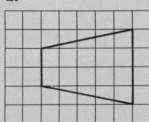

6.

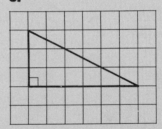

3.

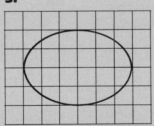

7.

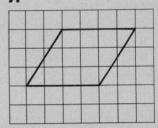

4.

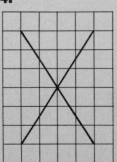

8.

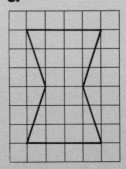

Chapter Fourteen

Squares and Square Roots

A. Squares

To square a number we multiply it by itself.
To square 4, we write it as 4^2. The small 2 tells you how many 4s are multiplied together.

So $\quad 4^2 = 4 \times 4 = 16$

And $(0.3)^2 = 0.3 \times 0.3 = 0.09$

Examples Square the following numbers: **(a)** 16 **(b)** 2.4

Solutions **(a)** $16^2 = 16 \times 16 = 256$

$$
\begin{array}{r}
16 \\
\times 16 \\
\hline
160 \\
96 \\
\hline
256 \\
\hline
{\scriptstyle 1}
\end{array}
\qquad
\begin{array}{r}
2.4 \\
\times 2.4 \\
\hline
480 \\
96 \\
\hline
5.76 \\
\hline
{\scriptstyle 1}
\end{array}
$$

(b) $2.4^2 = 2.4 \times 2.4 = 5.76$

Exercise 1 Square each of the following numbers:

1.	5	**8.**	10	**15.**	21	**22.**	0.6	**29.**	0.8
2.	6	**9.**	12	**16.**	30	**23.**	0.9	**30.**	0.03
3.	1	**10.**	11	**17.**	13	**24.**	1.2	**31.**	3.1
4.	8	**11.**	15	**18.**	14	**25.**	0.04	**32.**	26
5.	7	**12.**	20	**19.**	9	**26.**	1.1	**33.**	40
6.	3	**13.**	16	**20.**	25	**27.**	2.5	**34.**	1.3
7.	2	**14.**	18	**21.**	0.5	**28.**	1.6	**35.**	5.1

B. Square roots

The sign for square root is $\sqrt{}$

When we square a number, the square root of its answer is the same number that we square.

For example, when we square 4, the answer is 16. Therefore the square root of 16 is 4.

Similarly, $\qquad 3^2 = 3 \times 3 = 9 \quad \therefore \quad \sqrt{9} = 3$

The square root of 256 can be found by a trial and error method. That is, choose numbers and multiply them by themselves until you get 256. However, this is not a very powerful method for finding a square root, therefore we can adopt the method of continuous division using prime factors.

Method

Step 1. Choose prime numbers that can divide the number exactly.

Step 2. Divide until the answer is exactly 1.

Step 3. The square root is the product of *half* the factors that are alike.

Examples Find the square root of: **(a)** 256 **(b)** 324

Solutions

(a) $256 = 2 \times 2 \times 2 \times 2 \times 2 \times 2 \times 2 \times 2$

$\sqrt{256} = 2 \times 2 \times 2 \times 2$

$\qquad = 16$

We take 4 twos because there are 8 twos.

$$
\begin{array}{r|r}
2 & 256 \\
2 & 128 \\
2 & 064 \\
2 & 32 \\
2 & 16 \\
2 & 08 \\
2 & 4 \\
2 & 2 \\
\hline
 & 1
\end{array}
$$

(b) $324 = 2 \times 2 \times 3 \times 3 \times 3 \times 3$

$\sqrt{324} = 2 \times 3 \times 3$

$\qquad = 18$

We take 1 two because there are 2 twos.

And we take 2 threes because there are 4 threes.

$$
\begin{array}{r|r}
2 & 324 \\
2 & 162 \\
3 & 081 \\
3 & 27 \\
3 & 09 \\
3 & 3 \\
\hline
 & 1
\end{array}
$$

Exercise 2 Find the square roots of the following numbers, either using a trial and error method or using prime factors.

1.	4	**6.**	49	**11.**	225	**16.**	576
2.	25	**7.**	121	**12.**	169	**17.**	900
3.	36	**8.**	144	**13.**	100	**18.**	625
4.	1	**9.**	64	**14.**	441	**19.**	400
5.	81	**10.**	196	**15.**	484	**20.**	1600

Exercise 3 Complete these:

1. $16 = 2 \times 2 \times 2 \times 2$

$\therefore \sqrt{16} = \ldots$

$= \ldots$

2. $1225 = 5 \times 5 \times 7 \times 7$

$\therefore \sqrt{1225} = \ldots$

$= \ldots$

3. $676 = 2 \times 2 \times 13 \times 13$

$\therefore \sqrt{676} = \ldots$

$= \ldots$

4. $729 = 3 \times 3 \times 3 \times 3 \times 3 \times 3$

$\therefore \sqrt{729} = \ldots$

$= \ldots$

5. $784 = 2 \times 2 \times 2 \times 2 \times 7 \times 7$

$\therefore \sqrt{784} = \ldots$

$= \ldots$

6. $1024 = 2 \times 2 \times 2 \times 2 \times 2 \times 2 \times 2 \times 2 \times 2 \times 2$

$\therefore \sqrt{1024} = \ldots$

$= \ldots$

7. $\sqrt{6 \times 6} = \ldots$

8. $\sqrt{8 \times 8} = \ldots$

9. What number multiplied by itself gives 81?

10. What number multiplied by itself gives 144?

Chapter Fifteen

Indices

$16 = 2 \times 2 \times 2 \times 2$

This can be written as $16 = 2^4$. The raised 4 is called an *index* (the plural of index is indices). 2^4 is sometimes called 2 to the 4th power. The raised 4 also tells you how many twos are multiplied together.

Examples Write the following using index notation:

(a) $4 \times 4 \times 4 \times 4 \times 4$ (b) $a \times a \times a$

Solutions (a) $4 \times 4 \times 4 \times 4 \times 4 = 4^5$ (b) $a \times a \times a = a^3$

Exercise Write the following using index notation:

1. $2 \times 2 \times 2 = \ldots$
2. $3 \times 3 \times 3 = \ldots$
3. $5 \times 5 \times 5 \times 5 = \ldots$
4. $7 \times 7 \times 7 \times 7 \times 7 \times 7 = \ldots$
5. $b \times b \times b \times b \times b = \ldots$

Example Expand 4^3.

Solution $4^3 = 4 \times 4 \times 4$

Expand the following:

6. 2^6	10. 8^5	14. 8^3
7. 5^2	11. p^4	15. d^5
8. 4^4	12. y^7	
9. x^3	13. 9^2	

Examples   Find the value of: (a) 2^5 (b) $3^2 \times 2^3$ (c) $5^2 + 4^3$

Solutions   (a) $2^5 = 2 \times 2 \times 2 \times 2 \times 2 = 32$
(b) $3^2 \times 2^3 = 3 \times 3 \times 2 \times 2 \times 2 = 72$
(c) $5^2 + 4^3 = 5 \times 5 + 4 \times 4 \times 4$
$= 25 + 64$
$= 89$

Find the value of the following:

16. 2^2	**21.** 5^3	**26.** $5^2 \times 2$
17. 6^2	**22.** 4^4	**27.** $2^3 \times 3^2$
18. 4^3	**23.** 1^6	**28.** $4^2 \times 3^2$
19. 3^3	**24.** 10^3	**29.** $2^5 + 3^3$
20. 2^5	**25.** 7^3	**30.** $2^3 + 3^2$

Examples   Express the following in index form: (a) 27   (b) 100

Solutions   (a) $27 = 3 \times 3 \times 3 = 3^3$

$$\begin{array}{r|r} 3 & 27 \\ \hline 3 & 09 \\ \hline 3 & 3 \\ \hline & 1 \end{array}$$

(b) $100 = 2 \times 2 \times 5 \times 5 = 2^2 \times 5^2$

$$\begin{array}{r|r} 2 & 100 \\ \hline 2 & 050 \\ \hline 5 & 25 \\ \hline 5 & 05 \\ \hline & 1 \end{array}$$

Express the following in index form:

31. 8	**36.** 64
32. 32	**37.** 125
33. 25	**38.** 144
34. 40	**39.** 200
35. 75	**40.** 343

Chapter Sixteen

Bases Other Than 10

Our counting system is referred to as the *base 10* system. In base 10, we use the 10 digits 0, 1, 2, 3, 4, 5, 6, 7, 8 and 9 to form all the numbers that we need to write. There is no single digit to represent ten, eleven or any number greater than 9, therefore we have to use more than one of the above digits to do so.

Notice that in base 10 the number of digits we use does not exceed 10.

In base 8 there are 8 digits: 0, 1, 2, 3, 4, 5, 6 and 7
In base 5 there are 5 digits: 0, 1, 2, 3 and 4
In base 3 there are 3 digits: 0, 1 and 2
In base 2 there are 2 digits: 0 and 1

Base 10

$$6705 = 6 \times 10^3 + 7 \times 10^2 + 0 \times 10^1 + 5 \times 1$$

Base 8

$$6705 = 6 \times 8^3 + 7 \times 8^2 + 0 \times 8^1 + 5 \times 1$$

Notice that reading from right to left the first digit (5) stands for units, the second (0) for 8^1, the third (7) for 8^2 and the fourth (6) for 8^3.

Base 5

$$3241 = 3 \times 5^3 + 2 \times 5^2 + 4 \times 5^1 + 1 \times 1$$

Base 3

$$10211 = 1 \times 3^4 + 0 \times 3^3 + 2 \times 3^2 + 1 \times 3^1 + 1 \times 1$$

Base 2

$$110111 = 1 \times 2^5 + 1 \times 2^4 + 0 \times 2^3 + 1 \times 2^2 + 1 \times 2^1 + 1 \times 1$$

A. Changing other bases to base 10

Example (1) Change 476 from base 8 to base 10.

Solution

$$476_8 = 4 \times 8^2 + 7 \times 8^1 + 6 \times 1$$
$$= 4 \times 64 + 7 \times 8 + 6$$
$$= 256 + 56 + 6$$
$$= 318$$

or

$$
\begin{array}{ccc}
4 & 7 & 6 \\
\times 8 & +32 & +312 \\
\hline
32 & 39 & 318 \\
 & \times 8 & \\
 & \hline & \\
 & 312 & \\
\end{array}
$$

The subscript 8 in 476_8 shows that the number is a base 8 number.

Example (2) Change 431 from base 5 to base 10.

Solution

$$431_5 = 4 \times 5^2 + 3 \times 5^1 + 1 \times 1$$
$$= 4 \times 25 + 3 \times 5 + 1$$
$$= 100 + 15 + 1$$
$$= 116$$

or

$$
\begin{array}{ccc}
4 & 3 & 1 \\
\times 5 & +20 & +115 \\
\hline
20 & 23 & 116 \\
 & \times 5 & \\
 & \hline & \\
 & 115 & \\
\end{array}
$$

Example (3) Change 11110 from base 2 to base 10.

Solution

$$11110_2 = 1 \times 2^4 + 1 \times 2^3$$
$$+ 1 \times 2^2$$
$$+ 1 \times 2^1$$
$$+ 0 \times 1$$
$$= 1 \times 16 + 1 \times 8$$
$$+ 1 \times 4$$
$$+ 1 \times 2 + 0$$
$$= 16 + 8 + 4$$
$$+ 2 + 0$$
$$= 30$$

or

$$
\begin{array}{ccccc}
1 & 1 & 1 & 1 & 0 \\
\times 2 & +2 & +6 & +14 & +30 \\
\hline
2 & 3 & 7 & 15 & 30 \\
 & \times 2 & \times 2 & \times 2 & \\
 & \hline & \hline & \hline & \\
 & 6 & 14 & 30 & \\
\end{array}
$$

Exercise 1 Change the following base 8 numbers to base 10:

1.	16	**3.**	41	**5.**	60	**7.**	304	**9.**	1067
2.	25	**4.**	73	**6.**	127	**8.**	112	**10.**	4206

Change the following base 5 numbers to base 10:

11.	23	**13.**	20	**15.**	42	**17.**	204	**19.**	1023
12.	14	**14.**	34	**16.**	123	**18.**	143	**20.**	2134

Change the following base 3 numbers to base 10:

21.	11	**23.**	22	**25.**	102	**27.**	210	**29.**	2110
22.	12	**24.**	20	**26.**	212	**28.**	1210	**30.**	2012

Change the following base 2 numbers to base 10:

31.	10	**35.**	100	**39.**	11011
32.	11	**36.**	101	**40.**	101111
33.	111	**37.**	1011		
34.	110	**38.**	1111		

B. Changing base 10 numbers to other bases

Example (1) Change 79 from base 10 to 8.

Solution To do so, we divide 79 by successive 8s giving the remainder each time. The answer is then obtained from the remainders, starting from the last and reading upwards.

$$Ans = 117_8$$

$$
\begin{array}{r|l}
8 & 79 \\
\hline
8 & 09 \text{ R } 7 \\
\hline
8 & 1 \text{ R } 1 \\
\hline
 & 0 \text{ R } 1 \uparrow
\end{array}
$$

Read upwards

Check: $117_8 = 1 \times 8^2 + 1 \times 8^1 + 7 \times 1$
$= 1 \times 64 + 1 \times 8 + 7$
$= 64 + 8 + 7$
$= 79$

Example (2)   Change 268 from base 10 to base 5.

Solution

$$Ans = 2033_5$$

$$
\begin{array}{r|l}
 & \overset{2\,1}{268} \\
5 & \\
5 & 053 \text{ R } 3 \\
5 & 1^{1}0 \text{ R } 3 \\
5 & 02 \text{ R } 0 \\
\hline
 & 0 \text{ R } 2 \uparrow
\end{array}
$$

Read upwards

Check: $2033_5 = 2 \times 5^3 + 0 \times 5^2 + 3 \times 5^1$
$+ 3 \times 1$
$= 2 \times 125 + 0 \times 25$
$+ 3 \times 5 + 3$
$= 250 + 0 + 15 + 3$
$= 268$

Example (3)   Change 84 from base 10 to base 3.

Solution

$$Ans = 10010_3$$

$$
\begin{array}{r|l}
 & \overset{2}{84} \\
3 & \\
3 & \overset{-2-}{28} \text{ R } 0 \\
3 & 09 \text{ R } 1 \\
3 & 3 \text{ R } 0 \\
3 & 1 \text{ R } 0 \\
\hline
 & 0 \text{ R } 1 \uparrow
\end{array}
$$

Read upwards

Check: $10010_3 = 1 \times 3^4 + 0 \times 3^3 + 0 \times 3^2$
$+ 1 \times 3^1 + 0 \times 1$
$= 1 \times 81 + 0 \times 27 + 0 \times 9$
$+ 1 \times 3 + 0$
$= 81 + 0 + 0 + 3 + 0$
$= 84$

Example (4)   Change 39 from base 10 to base 2.

Solution

$$Ans = 100111_2$$

$$
\begin{array}{r|l}
2 & 3^{1}9 \\
2 & 19 \text{ R } 1 \\
2 & 09 \text{ R } 1 \\
2 & 4 \text{ R } 1 \\
2 & 2 \text{ R } 0 \\
2 & 1 \text{ R } 0 \\
\hline
 & 0 \text{ R } 1 \uparrow
\end{array}
$$

Read upwards

Check: $100111_2 = 1 \times 2^5 + 0 \times 2^4 + 0 \times 2^3$
$+ 1 \times 2^2 + 1 \times 2^1$
$+ 1 \times 1$
$= 1 \times 32 + 0 \times 16$
$+ 0 \times 8 + 1 \times 4$
$+ 1 \times 2 + 1$
$= 32 + 0 + 0 + 4 + 2$
$+ 1$
$= 39$

Exercise 2   Change the following base 10 numbers to base 8:

1. 12	**3.** 27	**5.** 71	**7.** 98	**9.** 370
2. 16	**4.** 50	**6.** 90	**8.** 209	**10.** 486

Change the following base 10 numbers to base 5:

| **11.** 9 | **13.** 26 | **15.** 81 | **17.** 218 | **19.** 483 |
| **12.** 18 | **14.** 75 | **16.** 106 | **18.** 390 | **20.** 627 |

Change the following base 10 numbers to base 3:

| **21.** 5 | **23.** 13 | **25.** 40 | **27.** 89 | **29.** 108 |
| **22.** 7 | **24.** 27 | **26.** 67 | **28.** 100 | **30.** 115 |

Change the following base 10 numbers to base 2:

| **31.** 3 | **33.** 7 | **35.** 11 | **37.** 21 | **39.** 47 |
| **32.** 5 | **34.** 9 | **36.** 15 | **38.** 34 | **40.** 65 |

Chapter Seventeen

Substitution

To substitute means 'to replace'.

If $n = 3$, what is the value of $4n$?

I must replace n by the number 3.

Now $4n = 4 \times n$

$ = 4 \times 3$

$ = 12$

$\therefore$ If $n = 3$, $4n = 4 \times n = 4 \times 3 = 12$

 If $n = 2$, $4n = 4 \times n = 4 \times 2 = 8$

 If $n = 1$, $4n = 4 \times n = 4 \times 1 = 4$

 If $n = 0$, $4n = 4 \times n = 4 \times 0 = 0$

Exercise Find the value of the following when $a = 2$:

1. $3a$ **2.** $4a$ **3.** $7a$ **4.** $8a$ **5.** $12a$

Examples If $x = 3$ and $y = 0$ find the value of:

(a) $xy + 6$ (b) $5 + 2x$ (c) x^2

Solutions

(a) $xy + 6$

$ = x \times y + 6$

$ = 3 \times 0 + 6$

$ = 0 + 6$

$ = 6$

(b) $5 + 2x$

$ = 5 + 2 \times x$

$ = 5 + 2 \times 3$

$ = 5 + 6$

$ = 11$

(c) x^2

$ = x \times x$

$ = 3 \times 3$

$ = 9$

If $p = 3$, $q = 2$ and $r = 0$ find the value of:

6. $p + q$ **10.** $pq + 4$ **14.** pqr

7. $p - q$ **11.** $6 + 3q$ **15.** $p^3 + q^2$

8. pr **12.** p^2

9. $p + q + r$ **13.** q^3

Examples   If $m = 3$ and $n = 4$ find the value of:

(a) $2mn$ **(b)** m^2n **(c)** $3n^2$ **(d)** $(3n)^2$

Solutions

(a) $2mn$
$= 2 \times m \times n$
$= 2 \times 3 \times 4$
$= 24$

(b) m^2n
$= m \times m \times n$
$= 3 \times 3 \times 4$
$= 36$

(c) $3n^2$
$= 3 \times n \times n$
$= 3 \times 4 \times 4$
$= 48$

(d) $(3n)^2$
$= 3n \times 3n$
$= 3 \times n \times 3 \times n$
$= 144$

Or **(d)** $(3n)^2$
$= (3 \times n)^2$
$= (3 \times 4)^2$
$= 12^2$
$= 12 \times 12$
$= 144$

If $a = 4$ and $b = 3$ find the value of:

16. $3ab$ **20.** ab^3 **24.** $a^2 + b^2$

17. a^2b **21.** $2a^2b$ **25.** $(a + b)^2$

18. ab^2 **22.** $(ab)^2$

19. a^2b^2 **23.** $3b^2$

Chapter Eighteen

Metric Units

A. Units of length

The basic unit of length in use today in many countries is the metre. A bigger unit than the metre is the kilometre, which is 1000 metres. Smaller units than the metre are the centimetre, which is $\frac{1}{100}$ of a metre, and the millimetre, which is $\frac{1}{1000}$ of a metre.

Table of length

10 millimetres (mm) = 1 centimetre (cm)

100 centimetres (cm) = 1 metre (m)

1000 metres (m) = 1 kilometre (km)

Units of length (smallest at the bottom)

kilometre

metre

centimetre

millimetre

If you look at your ruler, you will find that it is divided into centimetres. Each centimetre is divided into 10 mm.

Exercise 1 **1.** Look at the following lines. Then look at your ruler and *estimate* their lengths.

   (a) ——————

   (b) ———————————

   (c) ————————

   (d) —————————————

   (e) ————————————

   (f) ——————

2. Now use your ruler to *measure* each line and write down the measurement.

3. Measure these lines and give the answer in millimetres.

(a) ———

(b) ——————————

(c) —————

(d) ————————————

(e) ——————————

(f) —————————————

Changing from one unit to another

To change from a large unit to a smaller unit we multiply by 10, 100 or multiples of these.

To change centimetres to millimetres, multiply by 10. For example:

5 cm = 5 × 10 mm = 50 mm.

To change metres to centimetres, multiply by 100. For example:

2 m = 2 × 100 cm = 200 cm

To change kilometres to metres, multiply by 1000. For example:

2.5 km = 2.5 × 1000 m = 2500 m

Exercise 2 Complete the following:

1.	4 cm = ... mm		**16.**	1.6 m = ... cm
2.	6 cm = ... mm		**17.**	6.5 cm = ... mm
3.	3 cm = ... mm		**18.**	5.2 km = ... m
4.	2 m = ... cm		**19.**	16 cm = ... mm
5.	2 km = ... m		**20.**	6 km = ... m
6.	7 cm = ... mm		**21.**	4.2 km = ... m
7.	10 cm = ... mm		**22.**	3.9 cm = ... mm
8.	1.5 cm = ... mm		**23.**	10 m = ... cm
9.	3 km = ... m		**24.**	4.8 m = ... cm
10.	4 km = ... m		**25.**	13 cm = ... mm
11.	12 cm = ... mm		**26.**	30 cm = ... mm
12.	7.5 cm = ... mm		**27.**	8.5 km = ... m
13.	15 cm = ... mm		**28.**	14 km = ... m
14.	3.5 km = ... m		**29.**	16.8 cm = ... mm
15.	2.3 m = ... cm		**30.**	24.4 cm = ... mm

To change from a small unit to a bigger unit we divide by 10, 100 or multiples of these.

To change millimetres to centimetres, divide by 10. For example:

$60 \text{ mm} = (60 \div 10) \text{ cm} = 6 \text{ cm}$

To change centimetres to metres, divide by 100. For example:

$180 \text{ cm} = (180 \div 100) \text{ m} = 1.80 \text{ m}$ (decimal point moves two places to the left)

To change metres to kilometres, divide by 1000. For example:

$4200 \text{ m} = (4200 \div 1000) \text{ km} = 4.2 \text{ km}$ (decimal point moves three places to the left)

Exercise 3 Complete the following:

1.	8000 m = ... km	**16.**	850 cm = ... m
2.	2000 m = ... km	**17.**	28 mm = ... cm
3.	6000 m = ... km	**18.**	35 mm = ... cm
4.	20 mm = ... cm	**19.**	82 mm = ... cm
5.	40 mm = ... cm	**20.**	1750 m = ... km
6.	300 cm = ... m	**21.**	7000 m = ... km
7.	600 cm = ... m	**22.**	130 mm = ... cm
8.	1000 cm = ... m	**23.**	265 mm = ... cm
9.	120 mm = ... cm	**24.**	128 mm = ... cm
10.	180 mm = ... cm	**25.**	2425 m = ... km
11.	1200 m = ... km	**26.**	800 cm = ... m
12.	3600 m = ... km	**27.**	750 cm = ... m
13.	8400 m = ... km	**28.**	1500 m = ... km
14.	240 cm = ... m	**29.**	125 cm = ... m
15.	170 cm = ... m	**30.**	316 cm = ... m

Addition, subtraction, multiplication and division using units of length

Examples (a) Add

```
   m  cm
  13  47
+  8  96
  22  43
   1
```

As   100|143 cm

1 m 43 cm

(b) Subtract

cm mm
$_{10}$
18 3
− $\not{7}^{8}$ 7
10 6

(c) Multiply

m cm
4 38
× 4
17 52
$_{1}$

(d) Divide

km
$^{2\,2}$
5 ⟌ 3.7̇20
0.744

As 100 ⟌ 152 cm
1 m 52 cm

Exercise 4 Add

1.
cm mm
6 9
2 8
+ 5 6
‾‾‾‾

Add

2.
cm mm
8 4
1 0
+ 3 8
‾‾‾‾

Add

3.
m cm
4 27
12 60
+ 7 28
‾‾‾‾

Add

4.
m cm
6 48
3 37
+   89
‾‾‾‾

Subtract

5.
cm mm
10 2
− 3 7
‾‾‾‾

Subtract

6.
cm mm
16 0
− 6 8
‾‾‾‾

Subtract

7.
m cm
19 24
− 8 30
‾‾‾‾

Subtract

8.
m cm
27 33
− 16 48
‾‾‾‾

Multiply	Divide

9.   cm mm
      4   7
×   6
—————
	13. metres
	      6.04 ÷ 4

Multiply	Divide

10.   cm mm
      6   8
×   12
—————
	14. metres
	      17.2 ÷ 5

Multiply	Divide

11.   m   cm
     12 24
×   5
—————
	15. kilometres
	      27.640 ÷ 8

Multiply	Divide

12.   m   cm
     14 27
×   7
—————
	16. kilometres
	      318.5 ÷ 7

B. Units of mass

The popular units of mass in use today are the gram and the kilogram, where 1000 grams (g) = 1 kilogram (kg). There is, however, a bigger unit than the kilogram called the tonne, and a smaller unit than the gram called the milligram.

*Units of weight
(smallest at
the bottom)*

tonne

kilogram

gram

milligram

Table of weight

1 tonne (t) = 1000 kilograms (kg)

1 kilogram (kg) = 1000 grams (g)

1 gram (g) = 1000 milligrams (mg)

Changing from a big unit to a smaller unit

To change from kilograms to grams, multiply by 1000. For example:

$$2.5 \text{ kg} = 2.5 \times 1000 \text{ g} = 2500 \text{ g}$$

To change from tonnes to kilograms, multiply by 1000. For example:

$$5 \text{ t} = 5 \times 1000 \text{ kg} = 5000 \text{ kg}$$

To change from grams to milligrams, multiply by 1000. For example:

$$3 \text{ g} = 3 \times 1000 \text{ mg} = 3000 \text{ mg}$$

Exercise 5 Complete the following:

1.	3 kg	= ...g
2.	5 kg	= ...g
3.	8 kg	= ...g
4.	6 g	= ...mg
5.	2 g	= ...mg
6.	2 t	= ...kg
7.	7 t	= ...kg
8.	10 t	= ...kg
9.	8 g	= ...mg
10.	12 g	= ...mg

11.	14 t	= ...kg
12.	2.5 t	= ...kg
13.	5.6 t	= ...kg
14.	4.5 kg	= ...g
15.	6.8 kg	= ...g
16.	0.5 kg	= ...g
17.	0.8 t	= ...kg
18.	0.225 t	= ...kg
19.	0.75 g	= ...mg
20.	0.95 g	= ...mg

Changing from a small unit to a larger unit

To change grams to kilograms, divide by 1000. For example:

$$3500 \text{ g} = (3500 \div 1000) \text{ kg} = 3.500 \text{ kg} \quad \text{(decimal point moves 3 places to the left)}$$

To change kilograms to tonnes, divide by 1000. For example:

$$480 \text{ kg} = (480 \div 1000) \text{ t} = 0.480 \text{ t}$$

To change milligrams to grams, divide by 1000. For example:

$$5000 \text{ mg} = (5000 \div 1000) \text{ g} = 5 \text{ g}$$

Exercise 6 Complete the following:

1.	3000 g = ... kg		11.	4500 g = ... kg
2.	8000 g = ... kg		12.	2625 g = ... kg
3.	2000 g = ... kg		13.	600 kg = ... t
4.	5000 kg = ... t		14.	725 kg = ... t
5.	9000 kg = ... t		15.	150 mg = ... g
6.	4000 kg = ... t		16.	65 mg = ... g
7.	8000 mg = ... g		17.	320 g = ... kg
8.	7000 mg = ... g		18.	45 kg = ... t
9.	1400 kg = ... t		19.	30 mg = ... g
10.	1500 g = ... kg		20.	5 mg = ... g

C. Capacity

The basic unit of capacity is the litre. A smaller unit of capacity is the millilitre, which is $\frac{1}{1000}$ of a litre.

1000 millilitres (mL) = 1 litre (L)

To change millilitres to litres, divide by 1000. For example:
3000 mL = (3000 ÷ 1000) L = 3L.

To change litres to millilitres, multiply by 1000. For example:
1.6 L = 1.6 × 1000 mL = 1600 mL

Exercise 7 Complete the following:

1.	5000 mL = ... L	6.	2400 mL = ... L
2.	4000 mL = ... L	7.	3.4 L = ... mL
3.	12000 mL = ... L	8.	5.2 L = ... mL
4.	2 L = ... mL	9.	6500 mL = ... L
5.	6 L = ... mL	10.	450 mL = ... L

Exercise 8 Problems involving metric units:

1. A bag contains 50 kg of sugar. How many packets each holding 2 kg can be filled from it?

2. I have a piece of string 7.20 m long. If I cut a piece 54 cm from it, what length of string remains?

3. Divide 2.8 kg of cheese into 4 equal parts. What is the weight in grams of each part?

4. How many litres are needed to fill a container which holds 8000 mL?

5. How many litres of milk are needed to fill 12 bottles each holding 750 mL?

6. A girl's average step was 40 cm. How many metres would she walk in 200 steps?

7. Mr Browne the farmer sold 6 t of potatoes in bags each holding 100 kg. How many bags were there?

8. A piece of material 14.5 m long was cut into 5 equal pieces. What was the length in centimetres of each piece?

9. Mary is 1.65 m tall. Joan is 8 cm shorter. How tall is Joan?

10. A supermarket ordered 12 packets of butter each holding 25 kg. The butter was then placed in smaller packets each holding 500 g.

(a) What was the weight of the butter ordered?

(b) How many smaller packets were there?

11. How many half-litres of water would it take to fill a container which can hold $8\frac{1}{2}$ L when full?

12. How many pieces of wire each 6 mm long can be cut from a piece 9 cm long?

Chapter Nineteen

Measurement

A. Perimeter of closed figures

Remember The *perimeter* is the distance all round any closed figure. It is measured in long measure, e.g. centimetres and metres.

Example Find the perimeter of the figure to the right.

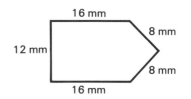

Solution Perimeter = 16 mm + 8 mm
+ 8 mm + 16 mm
+ 12 mm

= 60 mm

Exercise 1 Find the perimeter of each of the following figures:

1.

Rectangle   5 cm

8 cm

2.

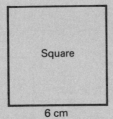

Square

6 cm

3.

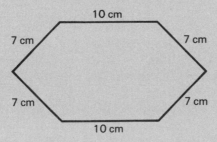

10 cm

7 cm   7 cm

7 cm   7 cm

10 cm

4.

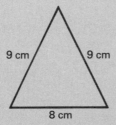

9 cm   9 cm

8 cm

5.

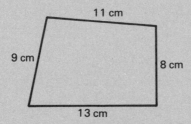

11 cm

9 cm   8 cm

13 cm

6.

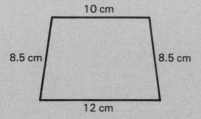

10 cm

8.5 cm   8.5 cm

12 cm

Example (1) The perimeter of a rectangle is 40 cm. If the length is 12 cm, what is its width?

Step 1. Draw a diagram of the rectangle.

Step 2. Put the measurements in the figure.

Step 3. Add the two lengths
12 cm + 12 cm
= 24 cm

Step 4. The two widths
= 40 cm − 24 cm
= 16 cm
∴ The width
= 16 cm ÷ 2 = 8 cm

12 cm

Rectangle

12 cm

Example (2) The perimeter of a square piece of card is 36 cm. Find the length of each side.

Each side = 36 cm ÷ 4 = 9 cm

Check: 9 cm + 9 cm + 9 cm + 9 cm
= 36 cm

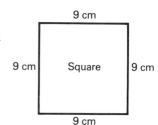

9 cm

9 cm   Square   9 cm

9 cm

Exercise 2   Complete the following table for a rectangle:

	Length	*Width*	*Perimeter*
1.	13 cm	8 cm	. . .
2.	15 mm	12 mm	. . .
3.	8.5 mm	6 mm	. . .
4.	7.5 m	8 m	. . .
5.	10 cm	6 cm	. . .
6.	7 cm	. . .	24 cm
7.	12 mm	. . .	40 mm
8.	. . .	5 cm	26 cm

Exercise 3 Complete the following table for a square:

	Length of side	Perimeter
1.	8 cm	. . .
2.	13 cm	. . .
3.	9.5 mm	. . .
4.	. . .	84 cm
5.	. . .	3.40 m
6.	. . .	100 mm

Example (1) The length of a rectangle is twice as long as the width. If the width is 7 cm, what is its perimeter?

Step 1. Draw a diagram of a rectangle.

Step 2. Put the measurements in the figure.
(The length is 7 cm × 2 = 14 cm)

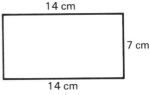

Step 3. Perimeter = 14 cm + 7 cm + 14 cm + 7 cm
= 42 cm

Example (2) The perimeter of the figure below is 35 cm. Find the measurement of the side marked x.

Step 1. Add the given measurements:
11 cm + 5 cm + 13 cm = 29 cm

Step 2. x = 35 cm − 29 cm
= 6 cm

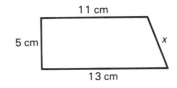

Exercise 4

1. Find the perimeter of a rectangle if the length is 14 cm and the width is 8 cm.

2. The length of a rectangle is 35 cm and the width is 16 cm. What is the perimeter?

3. Find the perimeter of a square piece of card of length 12 cm.

4. The perimeter of a square lawn is 172 m. What is the length of each side of the lawn?

5. The length of a rectangle is twice as long as the width. If the width is 8 cm, what is its perimeter?

6. The length of a rectangle is twice as long as the width. If the width is 12 cm, what is its perimeter?

7. The perimeter of the figure below is 59 mm. Find the length of the side marked *m*.

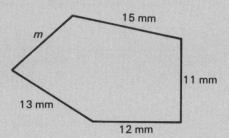

8. The perimeter of the figure below is 50 cm. The section ABCD is a square. The length of the curved part is 14 cm. What is the length of each side of the square?

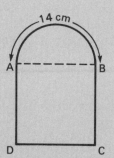

9. A boy ran all round a race track 3 times. If he ran 1200 m, what is the perimeter of the race track?

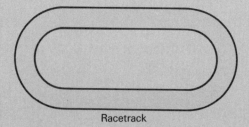

Racetrack

10. The distance all round a classroom is 18 m. The room is twice as long as it is wide. Find:

(a) its length   (b) its width.

B. Area of irregular shapes

An *irregular shape* is one whose dimensions cannot be determined. The two shapes below are irregular.

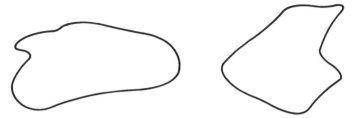

There is no method by which we can find the *exact* area of an irregular shape. However, we can find an approximate area of the shape by placing it on squared paper.

Method

(1)   Count the number of whole squares inside the shape.

(2)   Count the number of half squares, or squares which are bigger than a half square, inside the shape.

(3)   Add (1) and (2). This is an approximate area of the shape.

Example   Find an approximate area for the two shapes below:

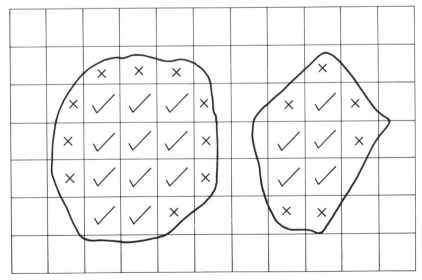

Fig. 1   Fig. 2

Area of shape (Fig. 1)

Number of whole squares $= 11$

Number of half squares or bigger $= 10$

Approximate area of shape (Fig. 1) $= 11 + 10 = 21$ squares.

Area of shape (Fig. 2)

Number of whole squares $= 5$

Number of half squares or bigger $= 6$

Approximate area of shape (Fig. 2) $= 11$ squares.

Exercise 5   Find an approximate area for each of the shapes below in square centimetres.

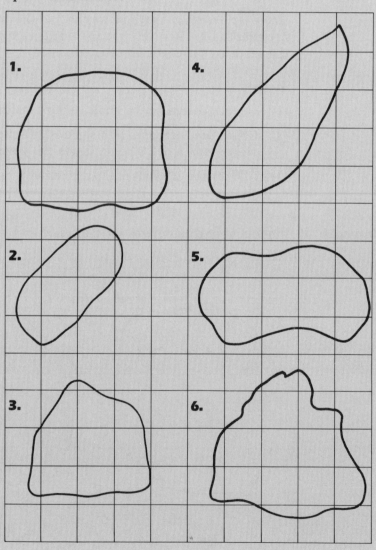

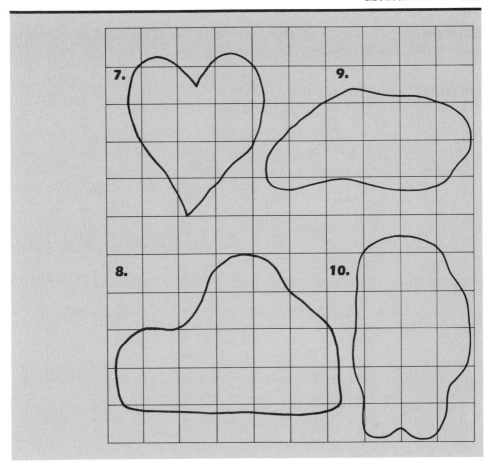

C. Area of rectangles and squares

Remember: Area is measured in square units, e.g. mm², cm², m².

Area = Length × Width
Length = Area ÷ Width
Width = Area ÷ Length

Example (1) Find the area of the rectangle.

Solution
Area = Length × Width
= 8.5 cm × 6 cm
= 51.0 cm²

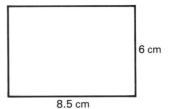

6 cm

8.5 cm

Example (2) The area of a rectangle is 108 cm². Find the width if the length is 12 cm.

Solution Width = Area ÷ Length
   = 108 cm² ÷ 12 cm
   = 9 cm

Exercise 6 Find the area of each of the figures below:

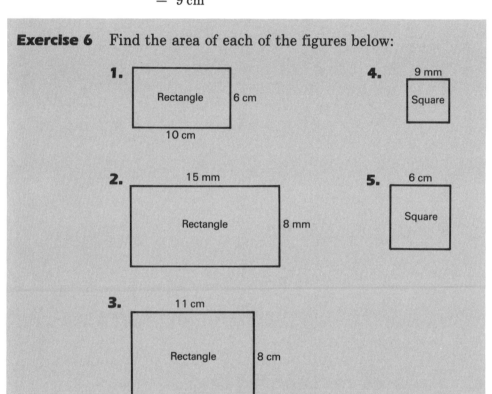

1. Rectangle 6 cm 10 cm

4. 9 mm Square

2. 15 mm Rectangle 8 mm

5. 6 cm Square

3. 11 cm Rectangle 8 cm

Exercise 7 Put in the missing measurements for a rectangle in the table below:

	Length	Width	Area
1.	8 cm	4 cm	. . .
2.	14 cm	8 cm	. . .
3.	10 mm	. . .	80 mm²
4.	. . .	4 m	60 m²
5.	12 cm	. . .	120 cm²
6.	. . .	5 cm	140 cm²

Example (1)   Find the area of a square whose sides are 14 cm long.

Solution   Area of square $=$ (Length)^2
$$= 14 \text{ cm} \times 14 \text{ cm}$$
$$= 196 \text{ cm}^2$$

Example (2)   Find the length of each side of a square if the area is 81 cm^2.

Solution   Length of each side of square $= \sqrt{\text{Area}}$ (square root of the area)
$$= \sqrt{81} \text{ cm}^2$$
$$= 9 \text{ cm}$$

Exercise 8   Put in the missing measurements for a square in the table below:

	Length of side	*Area*
1.	8 cm	. . .
2.	10 cm	. . .
3.	16 mm	. . .
4.	18 mm	. . .
5.	. . .	25 cm^2
6.	. . .	144 cm^2
7.	. . .	36 cm^2
8.	. . .	100 cm^2

Exercise 9

1. Find the area of a rectangular sheet of paper if the length is 9 cm and the width is 5 cm.

2. The length of a rectangular piece of card is 14 cm and the width is 8 cm. Find the area.

3. Find the area of a rectangle which measures 20 cm long and 12 cm wide.

4. The area of a rectangle is 100 cm^2. If the width is 5 cm, what is the length?

5. The area of a rectangle is 180 cm^2. If the length is 20 cm, what is the width?

6. The area of a square is 36 cm². Find the length of each side of the square.

7. The area of a square is 225 cm². Find the length of each side of the square.

8. The length of a rectangle is twice as long as its width. If the length is 18 cm, find the area.

9. How many tiles 6 cm by 6 cm would it take to cover a square floor whose sides are 360 cm long?

10. The perimeter of a square is 32 cm. Find its area.

D. Area of borders and shaded parts of squares and rectangles

Example (1) ABCD is a square whose sides are 4 cm long. P, Q, R, S are the mid points of each side of the square. Find the area of the shaded square PQRS.

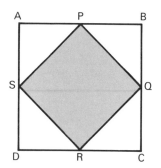

Solution

Step 1. Divide the shaded square as shown in the lower diagram.

Step 2. Area of square ABCD
   = 4 cm × 4 cm
   = 16 cm²

Step 3. Area of each shaded triangle
   = 16 cm² ÷ 8
   = 2 cm²

∴ Area of square
   PQRS = 2 cm² × 4
   = 8 cm²

($\frac{1}{2}$ area of square ABCD)

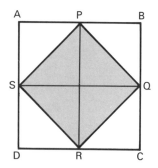

Example (2) Find the area of the shaded border in the figure below:

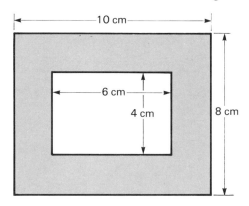

Solution
Step 1. Area of outer rectangle $= 10 \text{ cm} \times 8 \text{ cm} = 80 \text{ cm}^2$
Step 2. Area of inner rectangle $= 6 \text{ cm} \times 4 \text{ cm} = 24 \text{ cm}^2$
Step 3. Area of shaded border $= 80 \text{ cm}^2 - 24 \text{ cm}^2 = 56 \text{ cm}^2$

Exercise 10 Find the area of the shaded part of each figure below:

1.

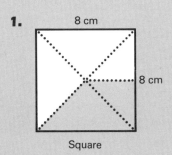

2.

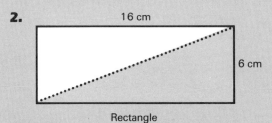

3. **4.**

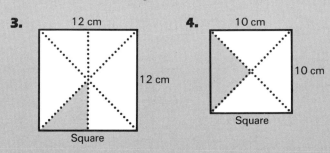

5.

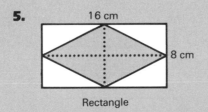

Rectangle

6.

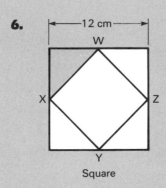

W, X, Y and Z
are the mid
points of each
side of the
square.

Square

7.

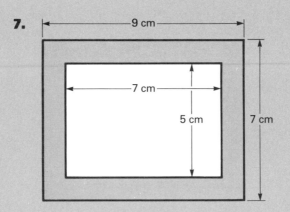

8.

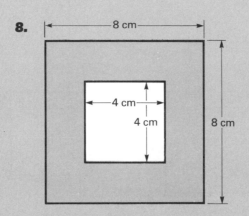

9.

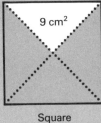

9 cm²

Square

10.

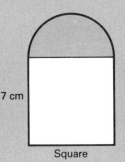

7 cm

Square

The area of this figure is 87.5 cm². What is the area of the shaded part?

E. Area of triangles

Look at the rectangle to the right.

Area of rectangle ABCD

= Length × Width

= 6 cm × 4 cm

= 24 cm²

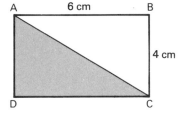

Area of triangle ADC (shaded)

= Half the area of the rectangle

$$= \frac{6 \text{ cm} \times 4 \text{ cm}}{2}$$

= 12 cm²

In the diagram above, DC is called the *base* of the triangle ADC and AD is called its *height*.

The height is a line perpendicular to the base. That is, the height forms an angle of 90° with the base.

The area of any triangle $= \dfrac{\text{Base} \times \text{Height}}{2}$

Examples   Find the area of the two triangles below:

1. 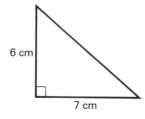   **2.**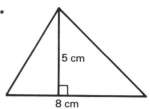

Solutions   **1.**   Area of triangle $= \dfrac{\text{Base} \times \text{Height}}{2}$

$= \dfrac{7 \text{ cm} \times 6 \text{ cm}}{2}$

$= 21 \text{ cm}^2$

2.   Area of triangle $= \dfrac{\text{Base} \times \text{Height}}{2}$

$= \dfrac{8 \text{ cm} \times 5 \text{ cm}}{2}$

$= 20 \text{ cm}^2$

Exercise 11 Find the area of the triangles below:

1. 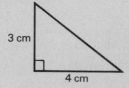   **3.**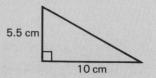

2. 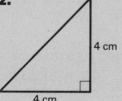   **4.**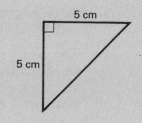

5.

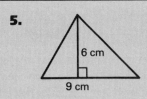

6 cm

9 cm

8.

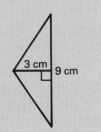

6.5 cm

10 cm

6.

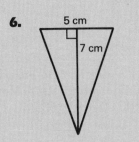

5 cm

7 cm

9.

3 cm   9 cm

7.

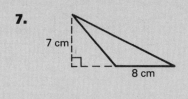

7 cm

8 cm

10.

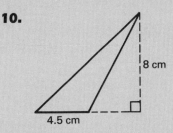

8 cm

4.5 cm

Find the area of the shaded triangles:

11. PQRS is a square of side 8 cm. A, B and C are the mid points of 3 sides of the square.

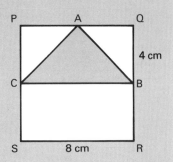

P   A   Q

C   B

4 cm

S   8 cm   R

12. DEFG is a rectangle. GF = 8 cm and EF = 6 cm.

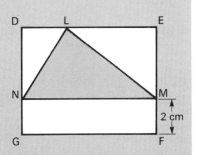

D   L   E

N   M

2 cm

G   F

F. Volume

The *volume* of a solid figure is the amount of space it occupies. Volume is measured in cubic measure because there are three dimensions. In this section we are only interested in finding the volume of cuboids and cubes.

1. Volume of a cuboid

The diagram below shows a cuboid 4 cm long, 2 cm wide and 3 cm high divided into cubic centimetres. How many cubic centimetres are there in this figure?

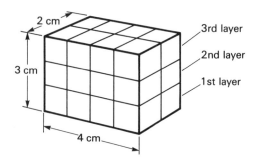

There are 3 layers with 8 cubes in each layer; that is, there are 24 cubes in the figure.

∴ 24 cubes or 24 cubic centimetres (24 cm³) is called the volume of the figure.

The volume can be found by multiplying length by width by height:

$$\text{Volume} = \text{Length} \times \text{Width} \times \text{Height}$$
$$\text{Volume} = 4 \text{ cm} \times 2 \text{ cm} \times 3 \text{ cm} = 24 \text{ cm}^3.$$

Example   Find the volume of a cuboid 6 mm long, 5 mm wide and 2 mm high.

Solution
$$\begin{aligned} \text{Volume} &= l \times w \times h \\ &= 6 \text{ mm} \times 5 \text{ mm} \times 2 \text{ mm} \\ &= 60 \text{ mm}^3 \end{aligned}$$

Exercise 12 Find the volume of each of the following cuboids:

	Length	Width	Height	Volume
1.	5 cm	3 cm	2 cm	...
2.	6 cm	5 cm	4 cm	...
3.	6 cm	4 cm	1 cm	...
4.	8 cm	5 cm	2 cm	...
5.	10 mm	6 mm	4 mm	...
6.	12 mm	8 mm	5 mm	...
7.	15 mm	12 mm	10 mm	...
8.	20 mm	12 mm	3 mm	...
9.	5 m	2 m	1.2 m	...
10.	4 m	2.5 m	0.8 m	...

2. Volume of a cube

Since a cube is a cuboid in which all the dimensions are the same, the volume of a cube $= (\text{Length})^3$

Example Find the volume of a cube of side 5 cm.

Solution

$$\begin{aligned}\text{Volume of cube} &= (\text{Length})^3 \\ &= (5\text{ cm})^3 \\ &= 5\text{ cm} \times 5\text{ cm} \times 5\text{ cm} \\ &= 125\text{ cm}^3\end{aligned}$$

Exercise 13 Find the volumes of the cubes with the following sides:

1.	6 cm	**5.**	10 mm	**9.**	12 cm
2.	4 cm	**6.**	7 m	**10.**	15 m
3.	3 cm	**7.**	0.5 km		
4.	8 cm	**8.**	0.3 km		

Example How many cubes of volume 2 cm³ would it take to fill a larger cube of side 4 cm?

Solution   *Step 1.* Draw a cube of side 4 cm.

Step 2. Divide the cube in cubes of side 2 cm.

The first layer requires $2 \times 2 = 4$ cubes

The second layer requires $2 \times 2 = 4$ cubes

$\therefore$ It would take $4 + 4 = 8$ cubes

Exercise 14 1. Draw a cube of side 6 cm. How many cubes of side 1 cm would it take to fill it?

2. Draw a cube of side 6 cm. How many cubes of side 2 cm would it take to fill it?

3. Draw a cube of side 8 cm. How many cubes of side 2 cm would it take to fill it?

4. Draw a cuboid 6 cm by 4 cm by 2 cm. How many cubes of side 1 cm would it take to fill it?

5. Draw a cuboid 8 cm by 4 cm by 2 cm. How many cubes of side 2 cm would it take to fill it?

6. Find the volume of a rectangular block 5 cm long, 4 cm wide and 4 cm thick.

7. How many cubic centimetres are there in a 7 cm cube?

8. How many cubes of side 4 cm could be cut from a cube of side 8 cm? (A diagram will help you.)

Example (1) Find the volume of a rectangular water tank 5 m long, 4 m wide and 80 cm deep. Give the answer in cubic metres.

Solution   Volume of tank $= 5 \text{ m} \times 4 \text{ m} \times 80 \text{ cm}$

$= 5 \text{ m} \times 4 \text{ m} \times 0.8 \text{ m}$ $(100 \text{ cm} = 1 \text{ m})$

$= 16.0 \text{ m}^3$

Example (2) Find the volume of a rectangular piece of lead 6 cm wide, 6 cm thick and 1 m long. Give the answer in cubic centimetres.

Solution   Volume of lead $= 6 \text{ cm} \times 6 \text{ cm} \times 1 \text{ m}$

$= 6 \text{ cm} \times 6 \text{ cm} \times 100 \text{ cm}$ $(1 \text{ m} = 100 \text{ cm})$

$= 3600 \text{ cm}^3$

Exercise 15 Find the volume of the following cuboids, giving your answer in the units in brackets:

	Length	*Width*	*Height*	*Volume*
1.	30 mm	20 mm	10 mm	$(\ldots \text{cm}^3)$
2.	50 mm	40 mm	20 mm	$(\ldots \text{cm}^3)$
3.	80 mm	60 mm	30 mm	$(\ldots \text{cm}^3)$
4.	500 cm	300 cm	300 cm	$(\ldots \text{m}^3)$
5.	600 cm	400 cm	200 cm	$(\ldots \text{m}^3)$
6.	2 m	3 m	250 cm	$(\ldots \text{m}^3)$
7.	3 cm	12 mm	8 mm	$(\ldots \text{mm}^3)$
8.	4 cm	10 mm	6 mm	$(\ldots \text{mm}^3)$
9.	36 cm	5 mm	8 mm	$(\ldots \text{mm}^3)$
10.	17 cm	100 mm	80 mm	$(\ldots \text{cm}^3)$

Example (1) The volume of a cuboid is 60 m³. If the length is 5 cm and the width is 4 cm, what is the height?

Solution

$$\text{Height} = v \div (l \times w)$$
$$= 60 \text{ cm}^3 \div (5 \text{ cm} \times 4 \text{ cm})$$
$$= 60 \text{ cm}^3 \div 20 \text{ cm}^2$$
$$= 3 \text{ cm}$$

Example (2) The volume of a rectangular block of wood is 600 cm³. If the width is 8 cm and the height is 5 cm, what is the length?

Solution

$$\text{Length} = v \div (w \times h)$$
$$= 600 \text{ cm}^3 \div (8 \text{ cm} \times 5 \text{ cm})$$
$$= 600 \text{ cm}^3 \div 40 \text{ cm}^2$$
$$= 15 \text{ cm}$$

Note: Width $= v \div (l \times h)$

Exercise 16 Find the missing dimensions for each of the following cuboids:

	Length	*Width*	*Height*	*Volume*
1.	6 cm	2 cm	. . .	24 cm^3
2.	. . .	3 m	2 m	60 m^3
3.	. . .	5 m	4 m	120 m^3
4.	12 mm	. . .	5 mm	600 mm^3
5.	6 m	4 m	. . .	72 m^3
6.	6 cm	5 cm	. . .	150 cm^3
7.	10 mm	. . .	5 mm	300 mm^3
8.	. . .	0.8 m	1 m	24 m^3
9.	. . .	4.5 cm	4 cm	198 cm^3
10.	8 cm	. . .	7 cm	448 cm^3

G. Time

Remember:

60 s = 1 min	$\frac{1}{2}$ min = 30 s	$\frac{1}{2}$ h = 30 min
60 min = 1 h	$\frac{1}{4}$ min = 15 s	$\frac{1}{4}$ h = 15 min
	$\frac{3}{4}$ min = 45 s	$\frac{3}{4}$ h = 45 min

Exercise 17 Complete:

1. 2 h = . . . min

2. 3 h = . . . min

3. 4 min = . . . s

4. $1\frac{1}{2}$ h = . . . min

5. $2\frac{3}{4}$ h = . . . min

6. 5 min = . . . s

7. $2\frac{1}{4}$ min = . . . s

8. 120 s = . . . min

9. 180 s = . . . min

10. 420 s = . . . min

11. 90 min = . . . h

12. 150 min = . . . h

13. 75 s = . . . min

14. 105 min = . . . h

15. $1\frac{3}{4}$ min = . . . s

Examples   (a)

	h	min
	3	46
+	2	75
	7	01
	2	

As   60|121 min
          2 h 01 min

(b)

	min	s
	15	20 (+60) 80
− 8	(7+1)	35
	7	45

(c)

	h	min
	3	16
×		4
	13	04
	1	

As   60|64 min
          1 h 04 min

(d)

	min	s
	5	11
6	31	6
−	30	+ 60
	01	66
×	60	− 66
	60	s 00

Exercise 18

1.

	h	min
	5	35
+	4	16

2.

	h	min
	3	18
+	1	14

3.

	h	min
	6	36
+	2	28

4.

	min	s
	2	26
+	3	40

5.

	min	s
	1	35
+	5	40

6.

	min	s
	3	8
×		4

7.

	min	s
	6	7
×		8

8.

	min	s
	2	10
×		7

9.

	h	min
	4	12
×		15

10.

	h	min
	3	11
×		7

11.	h	min	**13.**	h	min	**15.**	min	s
	8	25		10	15		7	20
	− 3	20		− 4	40		− 3	38

12.	h	min	**14.**	min	s
	9	40		6	30
	− 2	16		− 4	50

16. min s
8⟌24 40

17. min s
6⟌36 54

18. min s
5⟌26 00

19. h min
7⟌36 03

20. h min
9⟌20 06

Example A school lesson began at 9.30 a.m. and lasted for 40 min. At what time did it end?

Solution Since the lesson lasted 40 min, it must finish at a later time.

Therefore we must add 40 min to 9.30 a.m.

The lesson ended at 10.10 a.m.

	h	min
	9	30
+	0	40
	10	10

60⟌70 min
1 h 10 min

Exercise 19 **1.** A school lesson began at 8.45 a.m. and lasted for 30 min. At what time did it end?

2. A school lesson began at 9.00 a.m. and ended at 9.45 a.m. How many minutes did it last?

3. Joseph rode his bicycle from Bridgetown to Speightstown and took 25 min. If he started the journey at 7.40 a.m., at what time did he finish?

4. Our school starts at 8.40 a.m. One day a certain boy was 35 min late for school. At what time did he arrive at school?

5. Our school concert started at 2.15 p.m. The school choir was at the school 25 min earlier. At what time did the choir arrive at the school?

6. How many minutes are there between 11.45 a.m. and 12.20 p.m.?

7. Paul walks to school in 35 min. At what time must he leave home to arrive at school at 8.40 a.m.?

8. One night Mary spent 2 h studying. She spent 40 min doing comprehension, 45 min doing mathematics and the rest of the time doing English grammar. How many minutes did she spend doing English grammar?

9. John ran the half mile in 3 min. Samuel took 15 s less to run the distance. How long did it take Samuel to run the distance?

10. Mark ran the 10 km race in 1 h and 40 min. Ann took 25 min more to run the race. How long did Ann take?

H. 24-hour clock

You are quite familiar with times such as 1.30 p.m. and a quarter to eight. It is, however, modern practice to represent times by the 24-hour clock. The diagrams below show the relationship between the normal everyday 12-hour clock and the 24-hour clock:

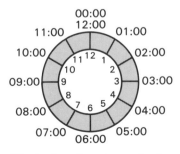

Clock showing times during the morning (a.m.) and at noon

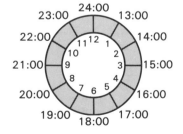

Clock showing times after noon (p.m.) and at midnight

Note that each 24-hour time is represented by 4 numbers. Two figures represent the hours and two represent the minutes. The hours are separated from the minutes by a colon(:).

Note too that for p.m. times, 12 h are added to the ordinary time to get the 24-hour time.

Examples   Write the following as 24-hour times:

(a)   8 a.m.   (b)   11.25 a.m.   (c)   1.30 p.m.

(d)   Half past 4 (p.m.)   (e)   A quarter to 9 (a.m.)

(f)   Five past 11 (p.m.)   (g)   Ten minutes to 12 midnight

(h)   Five minutes past 12 midnight

Solutions   (a)   8 a.m. is 08:00 hours.

(b)   11.25 a.m. is 11:25 hours.

(c)   1.30 p.m. is 13:30 hours.

(d)   Half past 4 (p.m.) means 4.30 p.m. which is 16:30 hours.

(e)   A quarter to 9 (a.m.) means 8.45 a.m. which is 08:45 hours.

(f)   Five past 11 (p.m.) means 11.05 p.m. which is 23:05 hours.

(g)   Ten minutes to 12 midnight means 11.50 p.m. which is 23:50 hours.

(h)   Five minutes past 12 midnight means 12.05 a.m. which is 00:05 hours.

Exercise 20   Write the following as 24-hour times:

1.	4 a.m.	**11.**	12.15 p.m.
2.	10 a.m.	**12.**	7.15 p.m.
3.	3 p.m.	**13.**	10.45 a.m.
4.	11 p.m.	**14.**	10.45 p.m.
5.	2.30 a.m.	**15.**	3.10 a.m.
6.	10.30 a.m.	**16.**	10.03 a.m.
7.	4.30 p.m.	**17.**	9.05 p.m.
8.	11.30 p.m.	**18.**	11.58 p.m.
9.	2.15 a.m.	**19.**	6.47 a.m.
10.	11.25 a.m.	**20.**	11.43 p.m.

21. Five thirty (a.m.)

22. Seven thirty (p.m.)

23. Eight minutes past three (p.m.)

24. Twenty minutes to midnight

25. Three minutes past midnight

26. A quarter past 5 (a.m.)

27. Twenty minutes to eight (a.m.)

28. A quarter past one (p.m.)

29. Half past three (p.m.)

30. Twenty-five minutes past ten (p.m.)

Examples   Write the following 24-hour times as ordinary 12-hour clock times:

(a) 03:15 hours   (b) 16:25 hours   (c) 00:15 hours

Solutions   (a) 03:15 hours is 3.15 a.m. or a quarter past 3 (a.m.).

(b) 16:25 hours is 16:25 − 12:00 = 4.25 (p.m.) or twenty-five minutes past 4 (p.m.).

(c) 00:15 hours is 15 min past midnight.

Exercise 21 Write the following as ordinary 12-hour clock times. Remember to put a.m. or p.m.

1.	09:45	**6.**	13:01	**11.**	03:25	**16.**	01:25
2.	05:10	**7.**	16:25	**12.**	01:04	**17.**	00:30
3.	07:30	**8.**	23:20	**13.**	21:30	**18.**	00:01
4.	10:05	**9.**	00:20	**14.**	20:15	**19.**	12:15
5.	12:40	**10.**	00:02	**15.**	19:20	**20.**	13:20

Example   A bus left Holetown at 09:45 hours and arrived at Speightstown at 10:05 hours. How long did it take?

Solution

The bus took 20 min.

Exercise 22 The table below shows the times a bus departs and arrives for different trips. Calculate the time taken in each case.

Trip	Departure	Arrival	Time taken
1.	08:00	08:40	. . .
2.	06:00	06:35	. . .
3.	09:30	10:00	. . .
4.	12:00	13:20	. . .
5.	13:15	14:00	. . .
6.	15:05	15:55	. . .
7.	16:25	17:10	. . .
8.	16:45	18:05	. . .
9.	20:10	21:05	. . .
10.	23:45	01:00	. . .

Exercise 23 Write, as 24-hour times, the time each clock is showing:

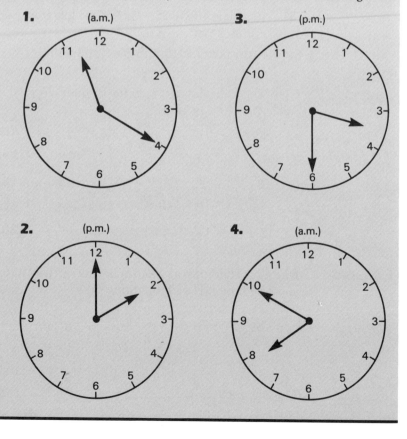

1. (a.m.)

3. (p.m.)

2. (p.m.)

4. (a.m.)

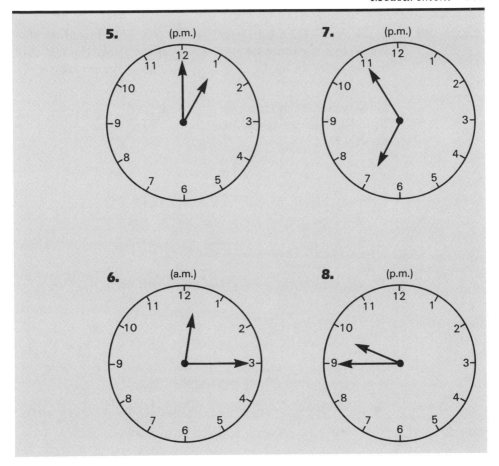

I. The calendar

Remember

7 days	= 1 week
365 days	= 1 ordinary year
366 days	= 1 leap year

Thirty days has September,
April, June and November.
All the rest have thirty-one,
Excepting February alone,
Which has but twenty-eight days clear
And twenty-nine in each leap year.

A *leap year* is one that can be divided exactly by 4.

Examples
Is the year 1990 a leap year? 4⌊$\overset{1}{90}$ (You need divide
No. Why? It cannot be $\overline{22\,R\,2}$ only the last two
divided exactly by 4.   figures by 4)

Is the year 2000 a leap year? 4⌊2000
Yes. Why? It can be divided $\overline{0500}$
exactly by 4.

Exercise 24   With or without the help of a calendar, answer the questions below.

1. How many Saturdays were there in the month of October 1985?

2. How many Mondays were there in the month of February 1986?

3. How many weeks were there from Monday 1st April, 1985 until Sunday 5th May, 1985?

4. 1984 was a leap year. **(a)** When will be the next leap year? **(b)** When was the last leap year?

5. How many days were there in February 1986?

6. How many days will there be in the year 1992?

7. How many weeks are there in 273 days?

8. How many days will there be in the year 1994?

9. 15th April, 1985 was a Monday. What date will be the next Monday?

10. This Saturday was the 18th May, 1985. What date was last Saturday?

11. Will the year 2006 be a leap year?

12. Today is Monday. Suzie's birthday is exactly 2 weeks away. On what day of the week will her birthday come?

13. On 12th June, 1985 Michael was 11 years and 7 months. When was he born?

14. Donna was born on 16th September, 1970. How old was she on 16th April, 1984? Give your answer in years and months.

15. How many days were there from 1st September, 1985 to 31st March, 1986?

J. Money

Remember: $1.00 = 100 ¢

Five dollars and three cents is written $5.03.

Five dollars and thirty cents is written $5.30.

Exercise 25 Addition

1.
$$\begin{array}{r} \$ \ \ ¢ \\ 13.56 \\ +\ 2.40 \\ \hline \end{array}$$

3.
$$\begin{array}{r} \$ \ \ ¢ \\ 74.85 \\ 32.17 \\ +\ 341.04 \\ \hline \end{array}$$

5.
$$\begin{array}{r} \$ \ \ ¢ \\ 183.80 \\ 241.48 \\ +\ 360.93 \\ \hline \end{array}$$

2.
$$\begin{array}{r} \$ \ \ ¢ \\ 38.09 \\ +\ 13.95 \\ \hline \end{array}$$

4.
$$\begin{array}{r} \$ \ \ ¢ \\ 337.46 \\ 120.75 \\ +\ 81.90 \\ \hline \end{array}$$

6. $94 + $72.45 + $0.70

7. $36.20 + $5.14 + $86.08

8. $70.75 + $12.78 + $2.03

9. $79.75 + $125.40

10. $64.45 + $6.28 + $19.97

Exercise 26 Subtraction

1.
$$\begin{array}{r} \$ \ \ ¢ \\ 8.40 \\ -\ 3.35 \\ \hline \end{array}$$

3.
$$\begin{array}{r} \$ \ \ ¢ \\ 89.36 \\ -\ 34.70 \\ \hline \end{array}$$

5.
$$\begin{array}{r} \$ \ \ ¢ \\ 114.08 \\ -\ 73.75 \\ \hline \end{array}$$

2.
$$\begin{array}{r} \$ \ \ ¢ \\ 71.65 \\ -\ 18.25 \\ \hline \end{array}$$

4.
$$\begin{array}{r} \$ \ \ ¢ \\ 646.20 \\ -\ 376.85 \\ \hline \end{array}$$

6. $19.60 − $12.40

7. $110.00 − $27.40

8. $480.75 − $98.86

9. $142.46 − $19.78

10. $124.00 − $74.72

Exercise 27 Multiplication

1. $8.40 × 4

2. $6.75 × 6

3. $8.24 × 7

4. $9.67 × 8

5. $15.73 × 9

6. $18.09 × 8

7. $26.48 × 10

8. $10.76 × 4

9. $13.76 × 6

10. $37.45 × 9

Exercise 28 Division

1. $9.40 ÷ 5

2. $76.24 ÷ 4

3. $48.40 ÷ 8

4. $36.33 ÷ 7

5. $118.70 ÷ 10

6. $328.44 ÷ 6

7. $430.50 ÷ 3

8. $315.76 ÷ 8

9. $643.50 ÷ 9

10. $843.80 ÷ 10

Exercise 29

1. Find the sum of five dollars and ten cents, sixteen dollars and eight cents, and ninety cents.

2. From eleven dollars and nineteen cents take four dollars and fifty cents.

3. How many five-cent pieces are there in twelve dollars and twenty cents?

4. How many twenty-five cent pieces are there in nineteen dollars?

5. An exercise book costs 85 ¢ and a pencil costs 16 ¢. What is the total cost of:
   (a)   4 exercise books and 2 pencils?
   (b)   6 exercise books and 3 pencils?
   (c)   7 exercise books and 1 pencil?
   (d)   12 exercise books and 4 pencils?
   (e)   3 exercise books and 7 pencils?

6. Last Saturday Mother spent $40.00 at the village shop. She spent $10.75 on vegetables, $7.20 on eggs and the rest on other groceries. How much did she spend on other groceries?

7. Mr Jones divided $35.20 equally among his 5 sons. How much did each son receive?

8. Which cost more and by how much: 6 shirts, each costing $25.75, or 4 pairs of pants, each pair costing $38.65?

9. Six (6) packets of sweet biscuits cost the same as four (4) chocolates. If a chocolate costs $4.80, what is the cost of a packet of sweet biscuits?

10. One quarter ($\frac{1}{4}$) of the money in my pocket is $12.00. How much money do I have in my pocket?

K. Foreign money

Foreign money is money that is different from our own local money. Money used by foreign countries like the United States of America, Canada and England is foreign to us.

Foreign money can be converted (exchanged) into Barbados money and back again. To carry out the conversion we use a figure called the *rate of exchange*. This figure is not fixed and may vary from day to day.

The rate of exchange for changing foreign money into Barbados money is always less than the rate of exchange for changing Barbados money into foreign money. This is to enable the bank carrying out the exchange to make a profit on the transaction.

In the examples and exercises below, Can. = Canadian, BB = Barbados and £ (pound) = English money.

To change foreign currency (money) to Barbados currency we multiply by the rate of exchange.

Example (1) Convert US $5.00 to Barbados currency when the rate of exchange is 1.98, i.e. US $1.00 = BB $1.98.

Solution As US $1.00 = BB $1.98

US $5.00 = BB $1.98 × 5.00

= BB $9.90

Example (2) Change £12 into Barbados currency, given that £1 = BB $2.60.

Solution   As £1 = BB $2.60

£12 = BB $2.60 × 12

= BB $31.20

Exercise 30 Complete the table below:

	Foreign currency	Rate of exchange	Barbados currency
1.	US $4.00	1.98	. . .
2.	US $6.00	1.98	. . .
3.	US $7.00	1.98	. . .
4.	US $10.00	1.98	. . .
5.	US $20.00	1.98	. . .
6.	Can. $10.00	1.40	. . .
7.	Can. $12.00	1.40	. . .
8.	Can. $15.00	1.40	. . .
9.	£10	2.60	. . .
10.	£40	2.60	. . .

11. Change US $15.00 into Barbados currency, if US $1.00 = BB $1.98.

12. How much Barbados currency is worth US $30.00, given that the rate of exchange is US $1.00 = BB $1.98?

13. Change £15 into Barbados currency when the exchange rate is 2.60.

14. If Can. $1.00 is worth BB $1.40, how much Barbados currency is worth Can. $20.00?

15. If a bank pays you BB $2.60 for £1, how much would you get for £20?

To change Barbados currency into foreign currency we divide by the rate of exchange.

Example (1) Convert BB $11.60 into Canadian currency if the rate of exchange is Can. $1.00 = BB $1.45.

Solution

$$BB\ \$1.45\ =\ Can.\ \$1.00$$

$$BB\ \$1\quad\ =\ Can.\ \frac{\$1.00}{1.45}$$

$$BB\ \$16.60\ =\ Can.\ \frac{\$1.00}{1.45}\times 11.60\ \left(\frac{1\times 11.60}{1.45}=\frac{11.60}{1.45}=8\right)$$

$$=\ Can.\ \frac{\$11.60}{1.45}$$

$$=\ Can.\ \$8.00$$

This is equivalent to simply dividing BB $11.60 by the rate of exchange, 1.45:

$$BB\ \$16.60\ =\ Can.\ \frac{\$11.60}{1.45}$$

$$=\ Can.\ \frac{\$11.60}{1.45}\quad (11.60\div 1.45\ =\ 8)$$

$$=\ Can.\ \$8.00$$

Example (2) How much in US currency can you get for BB $24.60 if the rate of exchange is US $1.00 = BB $2.05?

Solution

$$BB\ \$24.60\ =\ Can.\ \frac{\$24.60}{2.05}$$

$$=\ Can.\ \frac{\$24.60}{205}$$

$$=\ Can.\ \$12.00$$

$$\begin{array}{r} 12 \\ 205\overline{\smash{\big)}\,2460} \\ \underline{205} \\ 410 \\ \underline{410} \\ \overline{000} \end{array}$$

Exercise 31 Complete the table below:

	Barbados currency	Rate of exchange	Foreign currency
1.	$7.25	1.45	Can. $ . . .
2.	$14.50	1.45	Can. $ . . .
3.	$36.25	1.45	Can. $ . . .
4.	$8.20	2.05	US $ . . .
5.	$20.50	2.05	US $ . . .
6.	$32.80	2.05	US $ . . .
7.	$61.50	2.05	US $ . . .
8.	$26.50	2.65	£ . . .
9.	$106.00	2.65	£ . . .
10.	$137.80	2.65	£ . . .

11. Change BB $10.25 into US currency if the rate of exchange is US $1.00 = BB $2.05.

12. How much in US currency would you get for BB $30.75, given that the rate of exchange is US $1.00 = BB $2.05?

13. How much Canadian currency is worth BB $17.40 if Can. $1.00 = BB $1.45?

14. Convert BB $43.50 into Canadian currency if the rate of exchange is Can. $1.00 = BB $1.45.

15. How much in English money would you get for BB $53.00 if £1 = BB $2.65?

Given that EC $1.00 = BB $0.70:

16. How much BB currency is equivalent to EC $12.00?

17. How much EC currency is equivalent to BB $14.00?

Given that TT $1.00 = BB $0.30:

18. How much BB currency is equivalent to TT $50.00?

19. How much TT currency is equivalent to BB $36.00?

20. If US $1.00 = BB $1.98, how much BB currency is equivalent to US $60.00?

Chapter Twenty

Coordinates

Introduction

Points or positions in mathematics can be identified if the points or positions are placed on squared paper, as in the diagram below.

A. Naming points

In the figure to the right, $0x$ is called the x-axis and $0y$ is called the y-axis. The point where these two axes meet is called the origin. The name of this point is (0, 0) and we usually put the name in brackets.

Let us now name the point A.

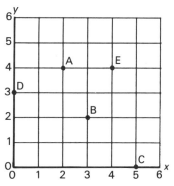

To do so, we look on the x-axis for the number that is in line with A; that is, 2. Thus, 2 is the first name, or x-coordinate, of A. Then we look on the y-axis for the number that is in line with A; that is, 4. Thus, 4 is the second name, or y-coordinate, of A. Therefore the name of A is, or the coordinates of A are, (2, 4).

Note that the x-coordinate always comes first. Similarly,

The coordinates of B are (3, 2)

The coordinates of C are (5, 0)

The coordinates of D are (0, 3)

The coordinates of E are (4, 4)

Exercise

1. Write down the coordinates of the following points as shown in the figure below: F, G, H, J, K, L, M, N, P, Q and R.

Begin like this: The coordinates of F are (0, 5).

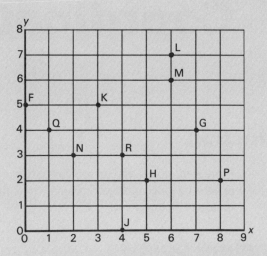

2. Using coordinates, give the positions on the map below of:

(a) Northpoint   (b) Farley Hill
(c) Harrison's Cave (d) The Barbados Museum
(e) Gun Hill   (f) Grantley Adams Airport.

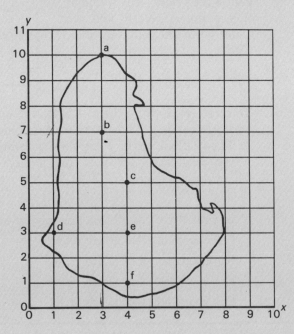

The *x*-coordinate of the point R (8, 2) is 8.

3. Write down the *x*-coordinates of the following points:

A (1, 7)   B (6, 4)   C (0, 5)   D (7, 0)   E (4, 3)

The *y*-coordinate of the point S (5, 6) is 6.

4. Write down the *y*-coordinates of the following points:

F (3, 4)   G (1, 3)   H (6, 0)   J (9, 6)   K (2, 5)

Look at the diagram below and then answer the questions.

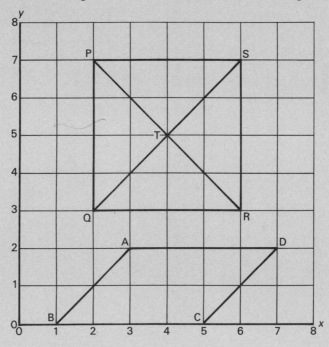

What are the coordinates of

5. P   **6.** Q   **7.** T   **8.** D?

9. Which point has coordinates (2, 3)?

10. Which point has coordinates (5, 0)?

11. What is the area of triangle QTR in square centimetres?

12. What is the area of figure PQRS in square centimetres?

13. What is the area of figure ABCD in square centimetres?

Select the name of a plane figure to name:

14. Figure PQRS   **15.** Figure ABCD.

16. Using numbers 0 to 12 on both axes, plot the following points on squared paper:

P (2, 5), Q (7, 3), R (1, 6), S (0, 4), T (6, 6), V (11, 9), W (8, 12), Z (8, 0).

17. **(a)** Using numbers 0 to 8 on both axes, plot the following points on squared paper: A (1, 2), B (4, 5), C (7, 2).

(b) Join these points to form a triangle.

(c) What is the area of this triangle in square centimetres?

18. **(a)** Copy the diagram below on squared paper and write down the coordinates of D, E, F and G.

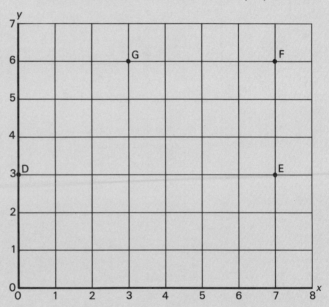

(b) Join these points in order, D to E, E to F, F to G and G to D to form a 4-sided figure.

(c) Select the name of a plane figure to name figure DEFG.

(d) What is the area of figure DEFG?

19. Using numbers 0 to 16 on both axes, plot the following points on squared paper to form quadrilaterals (4-sided figures):

(a) A (2, 9), B (8, 9), C (7, 11), D (4, 11)

(b) E (3, 5), F (6, 5), G (6, 8), H (3, 8)

(c) J (8, 5), K (13, 5), L (15, 8), M (10, 8)

(d) P (10, 9), Q (14, 9), R (14, 12), S (10, 12)

(e) T (1, 4), V (2, 2), W (5, 2), Y (5, 4)

(f) C (0, 11), D (2, 11), E (2, 14), F (0, 14)

(g) K (7, 4), L (7, 0), M (11, 0), N (11, 4)

(h) D (5, 14), E (7, 12), F (9, 14), G (7, 16)

20. Select names from the list (rectangle, square, parallelogram, rhombus, trapezium) to name each of the 4-sided figures you have formed.

Study the diagram, which is divided into square centimetres, and then answer the questions that follow:

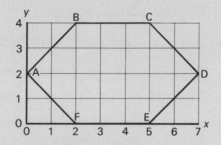

21. What are the coordinates of C?

22. What are the coordinates of E?

23. Which point has coordinates (0, 2)?

24. Which point has coordinates (5, 4)?

25. Which side is BC parallel to?

26. Which side is AF parallel to?

27. Name a horizontal line.

28. What is the area of this shape?

29. Name a line equal in length to FE.

30. How many right angles are formed with the six sides of figure ABCDEF?

Chapter Twenty-one

Averages

Here are 4 groups of marbles:

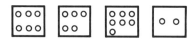

Each group does not have the same number of marbles.

Let us rearrange the marbles so that each group now has the same number of marbles.

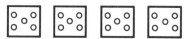

5 marbles are now in each group.

5 marbles is called *the average* of the marbles in the 4 groups.

Notice that some groups have more than the average and one has less than the average.

We could have calculated the average in the following way:

$$\text{Average} = \frac{\text{Total number of marbles}}{\text{Number of groups}} = \frac{20}{4} = 5 \text{ marbles}$$

Example (1)   Find the average of 7, 11, 6, 33 and 18.

Solution   Sum of numbers $= 7 + 11 + 6 + 33 + 18 = 75$

$$\text{Average} = \frac{75}{5} = 15$$

We divide by 5 because there are 5 numbers.

$$
\begin{array}{r}
7 \\
11 \\
6 \\
33 \\
18 \\
\hline
75
\end{array}
$$

Example (2)   Find the average of 12, 2, 17, 10, 31 and 0.

$$\begin{array}{r} 12 \\ 2 \\ 17 \\ 10 \\ 31 \\ 0 \\ \hline 72 \end{array}$$

Solution   Sum of numbers $= 12 + 2 + 17 + 10 + 31 + 0 = 72$

Average $\quad = \dfrac{72}{6} = 12$

We divide by 6 because there are 6 numbers.

Note that zero (0) is also a number.

Exercise

1. Find the average of 9, 7 and 5.

2. Find the average of 14, 6, 10, 3 and 2.

3. What is the average of 33, 8, 0 and 7?

4. A cricketer scored 19, 60, 39 and 22, in 4 innings. What was his average score?

5. Here are 6 numbers: 58, 44, 62, 31, 57, 48. Find the average of **(a)** the 3 smallest numbers **(b)** the 3 largest numbers.

6. What is the average of $12.50, $9.76 and $2.01?

7. The heights of 5 boys are: 1.65 m, 1.68 m, 1.57 m, 1.56 m and 1.74 m. What is the average height of the boys?

8. The table below shows the attendance for Class 4 for one week:

Days	Mon	Tue	Wed	Thurs	Fri
Pupils' attendance	26	31	29	32	24

What is the average attendance of the class?

Example   The average of 5 numbers is 13. Four of the numbers are 11, 9, 15 and 26. Find the fifth number.

Solution   *Step 1.* Sum of 5 numbers $= 13 \times 5 = 65$

Step 2. Sum of 4 numbers $= 11 + 9 + 15 + 26 = 61$

Step 3. Fifth number $= 65 - 61 = 4$

$$\begin{array}{r} 11 \\ 9 \\ 15 \\ + 26 \\ \hline 61 \end{array}$$

9. The average of 4 numbers is 20. Three of the numbers are 12, 18 and 28. Find the fourth number.

10. The average of 3 amounts of money is $7.05. Two of the amounts are $1.96 and $4.58. Find the third amount.

11. The average of 5 numbers is 20. Four of the numbers are 16, 9, 27 and 36. What is the fifth number?

12. The average of 6 measurements is 8.40 m. Five of the measurements are 4.36 m, 7.25 m, 6.10 m, 9.74 m and 11.35 m. Find the sixth measurement.

13. The average number of children in 2 groups is 26. If 6 children leave one of the groups, what is the new average?

Example The average of 2 numbers is 35 and the average of 3 other numbers is 40. Find the average of all 5 numbers.

Solution

Sum of 2 numbers $= 35 \times 2 = 70$

Sum of 3 numbers $= 40 \times 3 = 120$

Sum of 5 numbers $= 70 + 120 = 190$

Average of 5 numbers $= \dfrac{190}{5} = 38$

$$\begin{array}{r} 70 \\ + 120 \\ \hline 190 \end{array}$$

$$\begin{array}{r} 4 \\ 5\overline{|190} \\ \hline 038 \end{array}$$

14. The average of 2 numbers is 48 and the average of 2 other numbers is 26. Find the average of the 4 numbers.

15. The average of 3 numbers is 35 and the average of 4 other numbers is 21. Find the average of the 7 numbers.

16. The average of 4 measurements is 3.5 m and the average of 6 other measurements is 2.75 m. What is the average of the 10 measurements?

17. In 2 innings, a cricketer had an average of 50 runs. In 3 other innings, the cricketer had an average of 65 runs. What was his average for the 5 innings?

18. For the first 3 days of the week the average attendance for a class was 28. The average attendance for the next 2 days was 23. What was the average attendance for the 5 days?

Chapter Twenty-two

Unitary Method

Questions on this topic require you to find the cost of one article first.

Example (1) 5 similar pencils cost $1.20. How much would 8 of these pencils cost?

Solution

5 pencils cost $1.20

1 pencil costs $\dfrac{\$1.20}{5} = \$0.24$

8 pencils cost $0.24 × 8 = $1.92

First find the cost of 1 pencil.

1 pencil would cost less than 5 pencils, so divide $1.20 by 5.

8 pencils would cost more than 1 pencil, so multiply $0.24 by 8.

Or 5 pencils cost $1.20

1 pencil costs $1.20 ÷ 5

8 pencils cost ($1.20 ÷ 5) × 8

$$\dfrac{\overset{0.24}{\cancel{\$1.20}}}{\underset{1}{\cancel{5}}} \times 8 = \$1.92$$

Example (2) Find the cost of 10 similar pairs of socks if 3 pairs cost $15.

Solution

3 pairs of socks cost $15

1 pair of socks cost $15 ÷ 3

10 pair of socks cost ($15 ÷ 3) × 10 = $50

$$\dfrac{\overset{5}{\cancel{\$15}} \times 10}{\underset{1}{\cancel{3}}} = \$50$$

Exercise

1. If 5 similar exercise books cost $4.00, find the cost of:
   (a) 4 exercise books
   (b) 6 exercise books
   (c) 8 exercise books
   (d) 9 exercise books
   (e) 10 exercise books

2. Flying fish are sold at 5 for $1.00. Find the cost of 12 flying fish.

3. If a 2 L carton of milk costs $1.80, how much would a 5 L carton of milk cost?

4. A department store sells 3 metres of fabric for $15. How much would 5 metres of this fabric cost?

5. Mary exchanges 2 mangoes for 6 bananas. How many bananas would she get for 10 mangoes?

6. If 5 rulers cost $1.50, find the cost of 2 rulers.

7. 2 ballpoint pens cost just as much as 5 exercise books. How many exercise books would cost just as much as 6 ballpoint pens?

8. Find the cost of 20 sweets if they are sold at 2 for 5 cents.

9. 6 similar toys cost $21. How much would 8 of these toys cost?

10. A packet containing 3 tennis balls cost $7.50. What would a packet containing 5 similar tennis balls cost?

11. 2 similar boxes of crayons cost $6.50. Find the cost of 3 similar boxes of crayons.

12. 5 soft drinks cost $4.00. Find the cost of 8 similar soft drinks.

2 sheep are worth the same as 3 goats.

13. How many sheep are worth the same as 12 goats?

14. How many goats are worth the same as 10 sheep?

15. A box of biscuits cost $60.00. What will be the cost of 7 similar boxes of biscuits?

Chapter Twenty-three

Ratio

A. Meaning of ratio

Here are 5 circles, 3 shaded and 2 white.

The *ratio* of shaded circles to white circles is 3 to 2.

Look at these squares:

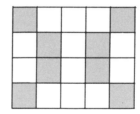

The ratio of shaded squares to white squares
is 8 : 12, or 2 : 3 (we divide 8 and 12 by 4)
    8 : 12 and 2 : 3 are *equivalent ratios*.

B. Dividing into a given ratio

Here are 15 pencils.
Divide them in the ratio
2 : 3.

How many are in each group?
The ratio of $2:3$ means that
each time you put 2 pencils in
one group, you must put 3 pencils in the other group.

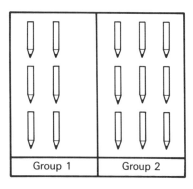

Group 1   Group 2

∴   6 pencils are in one group
and 9 pencils are in the
other group.

Example   Divide 60 marbles among 3 boys in the ratio $1:2:3$. How many
does each boy get?

Solution   No. of marbles to be divided $= 60$

Sum of parts $= 1 + 2 + 3 = 6$

1st boy gets $\frac{1}{6}$ of 60 marbles $= 10$ marbles

2nd boy gets $\frac{2}{6}$ of marbles $= 20$ marbles

3rd boy gets $\frac{3}{6}$ of 60 marbles $= 30$ marbles

$$\frac{1}{\cancel{6}}\times\frac{\overset{10}{\cancel{60}}}{1} = 10$$

$$\frac{2}{\cancel{6}}\times\frac{\overset{10}{\cancel{60}}}{1} = 20$$

$$\frac{3}{\cancel{6}}\times\frac{\overset{10}{\cancel{60}}}{1} = 30$$

Exercise 1
1. Divide 240 in the ratio $3:5$.

2. Divide \$120 in the ratio $3:4:5$.

3. Divide 45 into 2 parts in the ratio $7:8$.

4. Divide 70 into 3 parts in the ratio $1:2:4$.

5. Divide 40 plums between Ann and Sally in the ratio $3:2$.
How many plums does each girl get?

6. Share 63 apples among 3 boys in the ratio $2:3:4$. How
many apples does each boy get?

7. Divide \$3.00 in the ratio $3:7$.

8. Share 150 cherries among June, Fiona and Ruth in the
ratio $1:2:3$. How many cherries does each girl get?

9. Divide \$100 among 3 children so that when one child gets
\$2, another gets \$3 and the third child gets \$5. How much
does each child get?

10. Share 35 exercise books between 2 boys so that each time
one boy gets 3 books, the other boy gets 4 books. How
many books does each boy get?

C. Dividing or sharing so that one part is *x* times another

Example   Divide $30 between Mark and John so that John gets twice as much as Mark. How much does each boy get?

Solution   Since John gets twice as much as Mark, each time John gets $2, Mark gets $1. This is equivalent to saying that John gets 2 shares and Mark gets 1 share.

Money to be divided   = $30

Sum of shares = 1 + 2 = 3 $\frac{1}{\cancel{3}_1} \times \frac{\cancel{\$30}^{10}}{1} = \$10$

Mark gets $\frac{1}{3} \times \$30$ = $10

John gets $\frac{2}{3} \times \$30$ = $20 $\frac{2}{\cancel{3}_1} \times \frac{\cancel{\$30}^{10}}{1} = \$20$

Exercise 2
1. Divide 60 crayons between 2 pupils so that one pupil gets twice as many as the other. How many crayons does each one get?

2. Mr Brown had 120 pigeons. He divided them between his two sons so that one son got twice as many as the other. How many did each son get?

3. Divide 60 sweets between Sabrina and her sister Angela so that Sabrina gets thrice (3 times) as many as Angela. How many does each girl get?

4. Mother is twice as tall as her daughter Pam. The sum of their heights is 270 cm: **(a)** How tall is Pam? **(b)** How tall is her mother?

5. Pedro has 6 times as many marbles as his brother Carl. Together they have 70 marbles. How many marbles does each have?

D. Dividing so that one part is more than or less than the other

Example   Divide 80 ¢ between Sam and Carson so that Sam gets 6 ¢ more than Carson. How much does each boy get?

Solution   *Step 1.* Take out the extra share of 6 ¢.   80
          Step 2. Divide the remainder (74 ¢) into two   − 6
                 equal parts.   2⌊74
                 Carson gets one of these parts (37 ¢)   37
                 Sam gets 6 ¢ more (37 + 6) ¢   + 6
                 = 43 ¢   43

Exercise 3

1. Our teacher divided 30 markers between two boys so that one boy got 4 more than the other. How many markers did each boy get?

2. Divide $3.00 between Debra and Andy so that Andy gets 40 ¢ more than Debra:
(a) Debra gets . . .
(b) Andy gets . . . .

3. 35 pupils are in our class. There are 5 more girls than boys.
(a) How many boys are there?
(b) How many girls are there?

4. My sister and I picked 80 guavas. I picked 10 more guavas than her.
(a) How many guavas did I pick?
(b) How many guavas did my sister pick?

5. The sum of two numbers is 100. One number is 8 more than the other. What are the two numbers?

In a netball game, a total of 125 goals were scored. Team A scored 13 more goals than team B.

6. How many goals did team A score?

7. How many goals did team B score?

Auntie Kay divided 70 cherries between Esther and Ruth so that Ruth got 12 more cherries than Esther:

8. How many cherries did Ruth receive?

9. How many cherries did Esther receive?

10. How many cherries must Ruth give Esther so that both of them have the same number of cherries?

Chapter Twenty-four

Equations

An *equation* is a statement in which two quantities are equal. For example, all of the following statements are equations:

(1)	$3 + 2 = 5$	**(3)**	$2 \times 4 + 1 = 9$
(2)	$15 - 3 = 12$	**(4)**	$6 \times 6 = 36$

Examples   Find the value of x in the following equations.

(1) $x + 7 = 12$ *or*

$5 + 7 = 12$

$\therefore \ x = 9$

$x + 7 = 12$

$x + 7 - 7 = 12 - 7$

$\therefore \ x = 9$

(Subtract 7 from both sides of the equation)

(2) $6 + x = 15$ *or*

$6 + 9 = 15$

$\therefore \ x = 9$

$6 + x = 15$

$6 - 6 + x = 15 - 6$

$\therefore \ x = 9$

(Subtract 6 from both sides of the equation)

Exercise 1   Find the value of x in the following equations:

1.	$x + 5 = 7$		**9.**	$25 = 11 + x$
2.	$x + 3 = 10$		**10.**	$21 = 7 + x$
3.	$x + 4 = 15$		**11.**	$10 + x = 16$
4.	$x + 1 = 9$		**12.**	$9 + x = 9$
5.	$x + 6 = 12$		**13.**	$0 + x = 7$
6.	$18 = x + 10$		**14.**	$8 + x = 23$
7.	$20 = x + 12$		**15.**	$12 + x = 18$
8.	$13 = x + 10$			

Examples   Find the value of n in the following equations:

(1) $n - 5 = 12$ *or* $n - 5 = 12$

$17 - 5 = 12$ $\therefore n - 5 + 5 = 12 + 5$

$\therefore n = 17$ $\therefore n = 17$

(Add 5 to both sides
of the equation)

(2) $6 = n - 14$ *or* $6 = n - 14$

$6 = 20 - 14$ $14 + 6 = n - 14 + 14$

$\therefore 20 = n$ $\therefore 20 = n$

(Add 14 to both sides
of the equation)

Exercise 2   Find the value of n in the following equations:

1. $n - 4 = 7$ 9. $n - 13 = 7$

2. $n - 3 = 9$ 10. $n - 12 = 25$

3. $n - 8 = 11$ 11. $8 = n - 1$

4. $n - 5 = 5$ 12. $13 = n - 5$

5. $n - 6 = 12$ 13. $12 = n - 8$

6. $n - 4 = 0$ 14. $15 = n - 5$

7. $n - 0 = 8$ 15. $16 = n - 16$

8. $n - 7 = 17$

Examples   Find the value of a in the following equations:

(1) $2 \times a = 16$ *or* $2 \times a = 16$ (Divide both sides of

$2 \times 8 = 16$ $\dfrac{2 \times a}{2} = \dfrac{16}{2}$ the equation by 2)

$\therefore a = 8$

$\therefore a = 8$

(2) $5a = 30$ *or* $5a = 30$ (Divide both sides of

$5 \times a = 30$ $5 \times a = 30$ the equation by 5)

$5 \times 6 = 30$ $\dfrac{5 \times a}{5} = \dfrac{30}{5}$

$\therefore a = 6$

$\therefore a = 6$

Exercise 3 Find the value of a in the following equations:

1. $a \times 3 = 18$ 9. $28 = 2 \times a$

2. $a \times 6 = 6$ 10. $12 = 6 \times a$

3. $a \times 7 = 35$ 11. $3a = 36$

4. $a \times 4 = 40$ 12. $2a = 22$

5. $a \times 8 = 32$ 13. $5a = 45$

6. $36 = a \times 4$ 14. $12a = 120$

7. $50 = a \times 10$ 15. $10a = 70$

8. $63 = 7 \times a$

Examples Find the value of m in the following equations:

(1) $2m + 3 = 11$
        $2 \times m + 3 = 11$
        $2 \times 4 + 3 = 11$
        $\therefore\ m = 4$

or $2m + 3 = 11$
        $2m + 3 - 3 = 11 - 3$ (Subtract 3 from both sides of
        $2m = 8$ the equations)
        $2 \times m = 8$
        $\dfrac{2 \times m}{2} = \dfrac{8}{2}$ (Divide both sides of the
              equation by 2)
        $\therefore\ m = 4$

(2) $3m - 1 = 14$
        $3 \times m - 1 = 14$
        $3 \times 5 - 1 = 14$
        $\therefore\ m = 5$

or $3m - 1 = 14$
        $3m - 1 + 1 = 14 + 1$ (Add 1 to both sides of the
        $3m = 15$ equation)
        $3 \times m = 15$
        $\dfrac{3 \times m}{3} = \dfrac{15}{3}$ (Divide both sides of the
              equation by 3)
        $\therefore\ m = 5$

Exercise 4   Find the value of m in the following equations:

1. $2m + 1 = 7$
2. $2m - 2 = 8$
3. $3m + 1 = 13$
4. $4 + 2m = 8$
5. $1 + 5m = 11$
6. $2 \times m + 2 = 6$
7. $3 \times m - 1 = 8$
8. $2 \times m - 5 = 7$

9. $m \times 5 + 2 = 17$
10. $m \times 4 - 3 = 13$
11. $14 = 2m - 2$
12. $22 = 7m + 1$
13. $15 = 6m - 3$
14. $2m + m = 15$
15. $m + m = 16$

Examples   Find the value of d in the following equations:

(1) $$\frac{d}{4} = 6$$

$$\frac{24}{4} = 6$$

$$\therefore \quad d = 24$$

or $$\frac{d}{4} = 6$$

$$\frac{d}{4} \times 4 = 6 \times 4 \quad \text{(Multiply both sides of the equation by 4)}$$

$$\therefore \quad d = 24$$

(2) $$\frac{30}{d} = 10$$

$$\frac{30}{3} = 10$$

$$\therefore \quad d = 3$$

or $$\frac{30}{d} = 10$$

$$\frac{30}{d} \times d = 10 \times d \quad \text{(Multiply both sides of the equation by } d)$$

$$\therefore \quad 30 = 10 \times d$$

$$\frac{30}{10} = \frac{10 \times d}{10} \quad \text{(Divide both sides of the equation by 10)}$$

$$\therefore \quad 3 = d$$

Exercise 5 Find the value of d in the following equations:

1. $\dfrac{d}{2} = 6$ 6. $\dfrac{d}{8} = 4$ 11. $\dfrac{36}{d} = 9$

2. $\dfrac{d}{4} = 4$ 7. $\dfrac{d}{6} = 1$ 12. $\dfrac{16}{d} = 8$

3. $\dfrac{d}{2} = 9$ 8. $\dfrac{d}{3} = 0$ 13. $\dfrac{20}{d} = 4$

4. $\dfrac{d}{3} = 7$ 9. $\dfrac{16}{d} = 2$ 14. $\dfrac{28}{d} = 7$

5. $\dfrac{d}{6} = 6$ 10. $\dfrac{18}{d} = 6$ 15. $\dfrac{50}{d} = 5$

Examples Find the value of x in the following equations:

(1) $x^2 = 144$

$x \times x = 144$

$12 \times 12 = 144$

$\therefore \quad x = 12$

or $x^2 = 144$

$x \times x = 144$ (Find the square root of both sides

$\therefore \quad x = 12$ of the equation)

(2) $x \times x - 1 = 35$

$6 \times 6 - 1 = 35$

$\therefore \quad x = 6$

or $x \times x - 1 = 35$

$x \times x - 1 = 35 + 1$ (Add 1 to both sides)

$x \times x = 36$ (Find the square root of both

$\therefore \quad x = 6$ sides)

Exercise 6 Find the value of x in the following equations:

1. $x^2 = 9$ 4. $x^2 = 25$

2. $x^2 = 4$ 5. $x^2 = 100$

3. $x^2 = 16$ 6. $x \times x = 49$

7. $x \times x = 64$

8. $x \times x = 1$

9. $x \times x = 81$

10. $x \times x = 121$

11. $x \times x + 3 = 39$

12. $x \times x - 1 = 24$

13. $x \times x - 4 = 5$

14. $x \times x + 2 = 102$

15. $14 + x^2 = 15$

Exercise 7 Find the value of each letter in the following equations:

1. $a + 3 = 11$

2. $m - 2 = 8$

3. $x \times 3 = 24$

4. $n \times n = 4$

5. $\dfrac{d}{5} = 10$

6. $y + 7 = 15$

7. $x - 5 = 10$

8. $12 \times t = 48$

9. $2m - 1 = 11$

10. $6n = 42$

11. $(a \times a) + 3 = 19$

12. $c \times c = 225$

13. $t + t = 20$

14. $x - 5 = 8$

15. $8 - y = 2$

16. $12 + c = 19$

17. $8m = 40$

18. $28 = 2 \times y$

19. $20 = 5 \times a$

20. $t - 8 = 3$

21. $m + m + m = 24$

22. $16 - (a \times a) = 12$

23. $8 + (n \times n) = 17$

24. $x^2 = 196$

25. $3g - 4 = 11$

26. $14 - e = 4$

27. $(y \times y) + 3 = 28$

28. $6 + 3a = 12$

29. $5m - 2 = 13$

30. $y \times y = 400$

Exercise 8

1. 4 times a certain number is 48. What is the number?

2. What number divided by 5 gives 15?

3. If 8 is taken from 2 times a certain number, the answer is 18. What is the number?

4. 4 times a certain number plus 5 equals 37. What is the number?

5. What number must be added to the sum of 26 and 19 to give 60?

Chapter Twenty-five

Sets

A. Union of sets

The symbol for *union* is $\cup$.

$A \cup B$ means 'all the members from set A plus all the members from set B that are not in set A'.

Note that $A \cup B = B \cup A$.

Example (1) If $A = \{$cat, dog, rabbit$\}$ and $B = \{$sheep, goat, cow$\}$, then $A \cup B = \{$cat, dog, rabbit, sheep, goat, cow$\}$.

Example (2) If $D = \{$a, b, c, d, e$\}$ and $E = \{$a, e, i, o, u$\}$, then $D \cup E = \{$a, b, c, d, e, i, o, u$\}$.

Note that the members a and e are in both sets D and E and are not included *twice* in the set $D \cup E$.

Example (3) If $X = \{1, 2, 3, 4, 5\}$ and $Y = \{1, 2, 3\}$, then $X \cup Y = \{1, 2, 3, 4, 5\}$.

Exercise 1

1. If $P = \{1, 2, 3, 4, 5\}$ and $Q = \{6, 7, 8\}$, what is $P \cup Q$?

2. If $A = \{1, 3, 5, 7\}$ and $B = \{2, 4, 6, 8\}$, what is $A \cup B$?

3. If $R = \{1, 2, 3, 4\}$, $S = \{2, 3, 5, 7\}$ and $T = \{2, 4, 6, 8\}$, list **(a)** $R \cup S$ **(b)** $R \cup T$ **(c)** $S \cup T$.

4. If $M = \{$a, b, c, d$\}$ and $N = \{$a, b, e, f$\}$, list $M \cup N$.

5. If $C = \{$a, b, c, d, e$\}$, $D = \{$a, e, f, t$\}$ and $E = \{$h, l, m$\}$, list **(a)** $C \cup D$ **(b)** $D \cup E$ **(c)** $C \cup E$.

6. If F = {red, green, orange}, G = {red, white, blue} and H = {blue, gold, black}, list
   (a) $F \cup G$ (b) $G \cup H$ (c) $F \cup H$.

7. If A = {Saturday, Sunday} and B = {Tuesday, Thursday}, what is $A \cup B$?

8. If J = {3, 6, 9, 12}, K = {1, 2, 3, 6} and L = {2, 3, 5}, list (a) $J \cup K$ (b) $J \cup L$ (c) $K \cup L$.

9. If M = Whole numbers less than 6 and N = First 6 natural numbers, list (a) M (b) N (c) $M \cup N$.

10. If Q = {Odd numbers less than 10}, R = {Even numbers less than 10} and S = {Prime numbers less than 10}, list (a) Q (b) R (c) S (d) $Q \cup R$ (e) $Q \cup S$ (f) $R \cup S$.

B. Intersection of sets

The symbol for *intersection* is $\cap$.

Remember that the symbol for the empty set is { } or $\emptyset$.

$A \cap B$ means 'all the members of set A that are also members of set B'.

Note that $A \cap B = B \cap A$.

Example (1) If A = {mango, *cherry*, guava, plum} and B = {pear, apple, *cherry*}, then $A \cap B$ = {cherry}. (This is because cherry is in both sets.)

Example (2) If C = {a, b, c, d, e} and D = {f, g, h}, then $C \cap D$ = { }

Note that we use either { } or $\emptyset$ but not both; {$\emptyset$} is incorrect.

Exercise 2

1. If A = {car, bus, lorry} and B = {bicycle, motor-cycle, tricycle}, what is $A \cap B$?

2. If C = {red, green, blue, black} and D = {orange, yellow, pink}, what is $C \cap D$?

3. If G = {p, q, r, s, t} and H = {l, m, n, o, p, q}, what is $G \cap H$?

4. If J = {1, 2, 3, 4, 5, 6}, K = {1, 3, 5, 7, 9} and L = {2, 4, 6, 7, 8}, list (a) $J \cap K$ (b) $J \cap L$ (c) $K \cap L$.

5. If $L = \{1, 2, 3, 4, 5\}$ and $M = \{2, 4\}$, what is $L \cap M$?

6. If $P = \{7, 8, 9\}$ and $Q = \{1, 2, 3, 4, 5\}$, what is $P \cap Q$?

7. $R =$ Factors of 6 and $Q =$ Factors of 18, list
   (a) R (b) Q (c) $R \cap Q$.

8. If $S = \{$Multiples of 3 between 1 and 17$\}$ and $T = \{$Multiples of 4 between 1 and 17$\}$, list
   (a) S (b) T (c) $S \cap T$.

9. If $V = \{$First 5 whole numbers$\}$, $W = \{$First 5 natural numbers$\}$ and $Y = \{$First 5 odd numbers$\}$, list
   (a) V (b) W (c) Y
   (d) $V \cap W$ (e) $V \cap Y$ (f) $W \cap Y$.

10. If $A = \{$Prime numbers between 10 and 20$\}$ and $B = \{$Odd numbers between 10 and 20$\}$, list
   (a) A (b) B (c) $A \cap B$.

C. Problems based on Venn diagrams

Example (1) The diagram to the right shows a group of pupils from Class 4 where

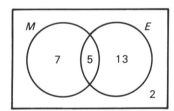

$M = \{$Pupils who like mathematics$\}$

$E = \{$Pupils who like English$\}$

Solution Here, 7 pupils like mathematics *only*.

5 pupils like both mathematics and English.

In other words, 5 pupils like mathematics and also English.

13 pupils like English only.

2 pupils like neither mathematics nor English.

$7 + 5 = 12$ pupils like mathematics.

$13 + 5 = 18$ pupils like English.

$7 + 5 + 13 + 2 = 27$ pupils are in the group.

Example (2) The diagram to the right shows a group of pupils where

F = {Pupils who play football}

T = {Pupils who play tennis}

V = {Pupils who play volleyball}

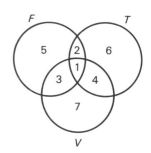

Solution Here, 1 pupil plays all three games.

5 pupils play football only.

6 pupils play tennis only.

7 pupils play volleyball only.

$(2 + 1) = 3$ pupils play both football and tennis.

$(3 + 1) = 4$ pupils play both football and volleyball.

$(4 + 1) = 5$ pupils play both tennis and volleyball.

$(5 + 2 + 6 + 3 + 1 + 4 + 7) = 28$ pupils are in the whole group.

Exercise 3   **1.** In Fig. 1:

E = {Girls who speak English}

S = {Girls who speak Spanish}

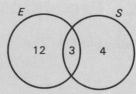

Fig. 1

(a) How many girls speak English?

(b) How many girls speak Spanish?

(c) How many girls speak both English and Spanish?

(d) How many girls speak English only?

(e) How many girls speak Spanish only?

(f) How many girls are in the group?

2. Fig. 2 shows a group of boys where each letter represents a boy:

C = {Boys who play cricket}

F = {Boys who play football}

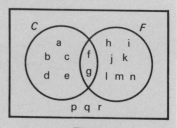

Fig. 2

(a) How many boys play cricket?

(b) How many boys play football?

(c) How many boys play both cricket and football?

(d) How many boys play cricket only?

(e) How many boys play football only?

(f) How many boys play neither cricket nor football?

(g) How many boys are in the group?

3. Fig. 3 shows a group of farmers where

$Y = \{$Farmers who plant yams$\}$

$C = \{$Farmers who plant corn$\}$

$P = \{$Farmers who plant potatoes$\}$

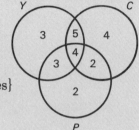

Fig. 3

(a) How many farmers plant all 3 crops?

(b) How many farmers plant potatoes only?

(c) How many farmers plant corn but neither potatoes nor yams?

(d) How many farmers plant yams?

(e) How many farmers plant both corn and potatoes?

(f) How many farmers are in the group?

4. In Fig. 4

$C = \{$Persons who drink coffee$\}$

$T = \{$Persons who drink tea$\}$,

and each small letter represents a person.

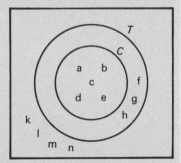

Fig. 4

(a) How many persons drink tea?

(b) How many persons drink coffee?

(c) How many persons drink tea only?

(d) How many persons drink neither coffee nor tea?

(e) How many persons drink both coffee and tea?

5. In Fig. 5

$E = \{$Houses that have electricity$\}$

$T = \{$Houses that have telephones$\}$

$W = \{$Houses that have water$\}$

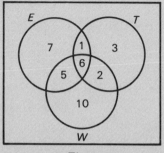

Fig. 5

(a) How many houses have electricity?

(b) How many houses have water only?

(c) How many houses have electricity and water but not telephones?

(d) How many houses have both water and telephone?

(e) How many houses do not have telephones?

(f) How many houses have electricity and telephones as well as water?

(g) How many houses have electricity but neither telephones nor water?

(h) How many houses are there altogether?

Chapter Twenty-six

Distance, Speed and Time

A. Meaning of metres per second and kilometres per hour

Metres per second means the number of metres travelled in 1 s. Kilometres per hour means the number of kilometres travelled in 1 h.

'A bus was travelling at 60 kilometres per hour' means that the bus could travel 60 km in 1 h.

'An athlete was running at 10 metres per second' means that the athlete could run 10 m in 1 s.

B. Problems involving distance, speed and time

Example (1) An aircraft travelled 4000 km in 5 h. What was its average speed?

In other words, how far did the aircraft travel in 1 h?

Solution
In 5 h aircraft travelled 4000 km

$\therefore$ In 1 h aircraft travelled 4000 km $\div$ 5 $=$ 800 km

$\therefore$ Average speed $=$ 800 km per hour

Average speed $=$ Distance $\div$ Time

Example (2) A car travelled at an average speed of 80 km per hour for 4 h. How far did it travel?

Solution

In 1 h car travelled 80 km

∴ In 4 h car travelled 80 km × 4 = 320 km

Distance = Speed × Time

Example (3) A cyclist travelled for 4000 m at a speed of 25 m per second. How long did the distance take?

Solution

25 m took 1 s

1 m took $\dfrac{1}{25}$ s

4000 m took $\dfrac{1}{25}$ × 4000 s $\dfrac{1}{\cancel{25}_1} \times \dfrac{\overset{160}{\cancel{4000}}}{1} = 160$

=160 s

Or all we need to find is how many 25 m there are in 4000 m.

$$\text{Time taken } = \frac{4000 \text{ m}}{25 \text{ m per second}} = 160 \text{ s}$$

Time = Distance ÷ Speed

Exercise Complete this table:

	Distance	Time	Speed
1.	. . .	3 h	70 km per hour
2.	. . .	5 h	45 km per hour
3.	280 km	. . .	40 km per hour
4.	450 m	15 s	. . .
5.	. . .	$2\frac{1}{2}$ s	60 m per second
6.	5000 km	8 h	. . .
7.	. . .	$2\frac{1}{2}$ h	80 km per hour
8.	1000 m	. . .	25 m per second
9.	6000 m	. . .	120 m per second
10.	40 km	2 h 40 min	. . .

11. A car travels at 75 km per hour:

    (a) How far will it travel in 3 h at the same rate?

    (b) How far will it travel in 15 min at the same rate

    (c) How long will it take to travel 150 km?

12. A cyclist travelled 800 m in 32 s. What was his speed in metres per second?

13. A bus travelled 200 km at an average speed of 50 km per hour. How long did the distance take?

14. Tom can cycle at a speed of 24 km per hour. It takes him 10 min to get to school. How far from the school does he live?

15. An aircraft travels at 800 km per hour.

    (a) How far would it travel in 15 min?

    (b) How long would it take to travel 2000 km?

A boy can cycle at an average speed of 20 km per hour, at that rate:

16. How far can he cycle in 2 h?

17. How far can he cycle in 3 h?

18. How far can he cycle in 15 min?

19. How long would it take him to cycle 80 km?

20. How long would it take him to cycle 90 km?

Chapter Twenty-seven

Graphs

Introduction

A group of 36 pupils were asked to write down the name of their favourite TV programme and the responses were as follows:

Dallas	6	*Hawaii Five-O*	3
Days of Our Lives	5	*The Jeffersons*	9
Knight Rider	12	*Spiderman*	1

This information can also be presented by means of a *graph*. A graph is a picture which allows one to read information easily and quickly.

Let us now represent the same information above by four different graphs.

A. The pictograph

A *pictograph* showing the favourite TV programme for a group of 36 pupils:

represents 1 pupil

TV PROGRAMME	PUPILS
Dallas	👤👤👤👤👤👤
Days of Our Lives	👤👤👤👤👤
Knight Rider	👤👤👤👤👤👤👤👤👤👤👤👤
Hawaii Five-O	👤👤👤
The Jeffersons	👤👤👤👤👤👤👤👤👤
Spiderman	👤

B. The line graph

A *line graph* showing the favourite TV programme for a group of 36 pupils:

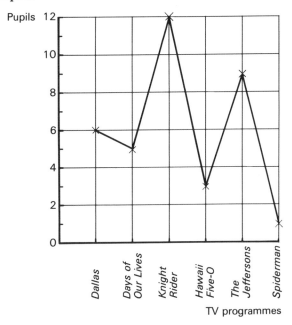

C. The bar chart

Bar charts showing the favourite TV programme for a group of 36 pupils:

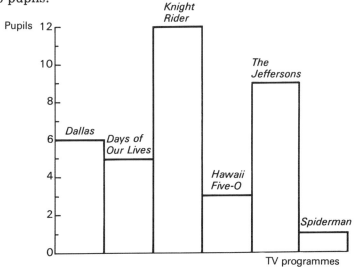

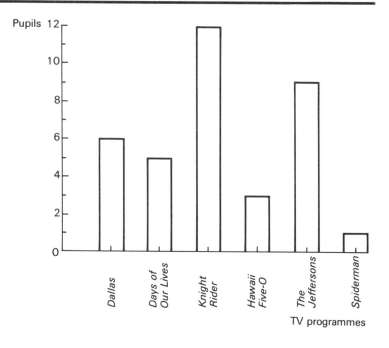

D. The pie chart

The *pie chart* is circular in shape. Let us find out how many degrees each item should occupy.

First we add the number of items:
Number of pupils $= 6 + 5 + 12 + 3 + 9 + 1 = 36$

Since there are 360° in a circle,
each item is represented by 360° ÷ 36 $= 10°$
6 items are represented by $10° \times 6 = 60°$ (*Dallas*)
5 items are represented by $10° \times 5 = 50°$ (*Days of Our Lives*)
12 items are represented by $10° \times 12 = 120°$ (*Knight Rider*)
3 items are represented by $10° \times 3 = 30°$ (*Hawaii Five-O*)
9 items are represented by $10° \times 9 = 90°$ (*The Jeffersons*)
1 item is represented by $10° \times 1 = 10°$ (*Spiderman*)

A pie chart showing the favourite TV programme for a group of 36 pupils:

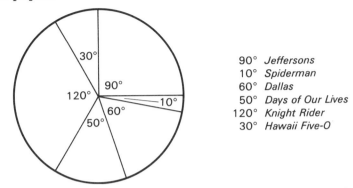

90° *Jeffersons*
10° *Spiderman*
60° *Dallas*
50° *Days of Our Lives*
120° *Knight Rider*
30° *Hawaii Five-O*

Example (1) The graph the below shows the time taken by 5 eleven-year-old boys to run the 100 m.

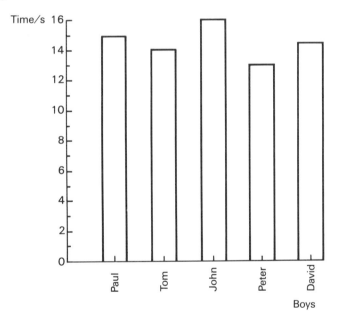

(a) Who was the fastest runner?
   (Peter)

(b) Who was the slowest runner?
   (John)

(c) How many seconds did Tom take to run the 100 m?
   (14 s)

(d) How many boys ran the 100 m faster than Paul?
   (3 boys)

Example (2) The pie chart to below shows the favourite colour of the 24 girls from Class 4:

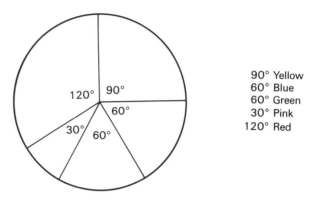

90° Yellow
60° Blue
60° Green
30° Pink
120° Red

(a) How many girls like yellow?

$$Ans = \frac{90°}{360°} \times 24$$

$$= 6 \text{ girls}$$

(b) How many girls like red?

$$Ans = \frac{120°}{360°} \times 24$$

$$= 8 \text{ girls}$$

(c) Which two colours are equally popular?

$$Ans = \text{Green and blue}$$

Exercise **1.** The pictograph below shows the favourite subjects for a certain Junior class.

👤 represents 1 pupil

SUBJECTS	PUPILS
Art	👤 👤 👤 👤 👤 👤 👤 👤 👤
English	👤 👤 👤 👤 👤 👤
Mathematics	👤 👤 👤
Science	👤 👤 👤 👤 👤 👤
Scripture	👤 👤
Social Studies	👤 👤 👤 👤

(a) How many pupils like social studies?

(b) Which subject is the most popular?

(c) How many more pupils like English than scripture?

(d) Which two subjects are equally popular?

(e) How many pupils are in the Junior class?

2. The graph shows the times taken by 5 cyclists to ride around a 400 m race track once only.

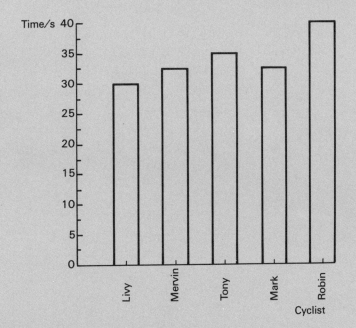

(a) Who was the slowest rider?

(b) Who was the fastest rider?

(c) How long did Livy take to ride the distance?

(d) Which two riders took the same time to ride the distance?

(e) What was Robin's speed in metres per second?

3. The pie chart shows the different ways a group of 48 pupils come to school.

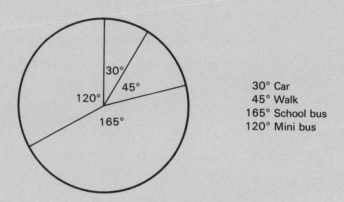

30° Car
45° Walk
165° School bus
120° Mini bus

(a) How many pupils come to school by the school bus?

(b) How many pupils walk to school?

(c) Which way is the *least* popular way of coming to school?

(d) What fraction of the pupils use the minibus?

4. The graph shows the rainfall in millimetres for the last 6 months of a certain year.

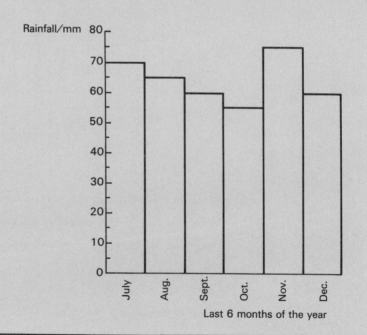

(a) How many millimetres of rain fell in July?

(b) Which month was wettest?

(c) Which month was driest?

(d) In which two months did the same amount of rain fall?

(e) What was the average rainfall for the 6 month period?

5. 30 pupils are in Class 4. The graph shows their attendance for a 5-day week.

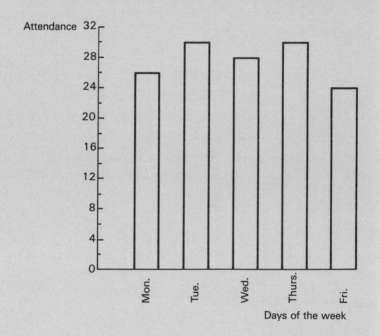

(a) How many pupils came to school on Wednesday?

(b) On which day did all the pupils come to school?

(c) On which day did the least number of pupils come to school?

(d) How many pupils were absent on Monday?

(e) What was the average attendance for the week?

6. The graph shows the scores of a cricketer in his first 5 innings of the season.

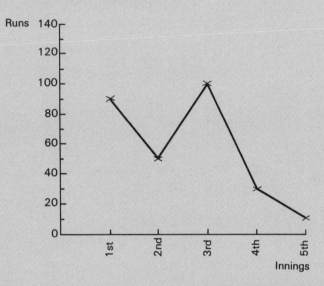

(a) How many runs did he make in his first innings?

(b) In which innings did he make the highest score?

(c) In which innings did he make 30 runs?

(d) What was his total runs for the 5 innings?

(e) What was his average score for the 5 innings?

Chapter Twenty-eight

Scale Drawing

Introduction

Can you draw the size of your school on a page of your exercise book?

Can you draw the size of your form room on a page of your exercise book?

Can you draw the size of your desk-top on a page of your exercise book?

If the answer to each of these questions is no, then we need to know how to represent the above sizes on a page of your exercise book.

Scale drawing is a way of representing long measurements by short measurements, and large sizes by small sizes.

Suppose that your form room is 8 m long and 6 m wide, we can use scale drawing to represent the size of its floor on paper. We can say, let 1 cm represent 1 m, or let 1 cm represent 2 m.

The following diagrams show scale drawings of the floor of a form room 8 m long and 6 m wide.

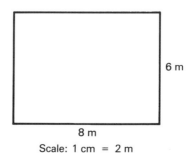

6 m

8 m

Scale: 1 cm = 2 m

6 m

8 m

Scale: 1 cm = 1 m

Example (1)   Using the scale 1 cm = 1 m, what are the lengths in metres of the following lines?

A ———————————————— B

C ——————————— D

Solution   First measure the lines in centimetres:

AB measures 5 cm   CD measures 4.5 cm

1 cm = 1 m   1 cm = 1 m

∴   5 cm = 1 m × 5 = 5 m   4.5 cm = 1 m × 4.5

∴   AB is 5 m   = 4.5 m

                                    ∴   CD is 4.5 m

Example (2)   Using the scale 1 cm = 5 m, what are the lengths in metres of the following lines?

P ———————————————————— Q

M ————————————— N

Solution   First measure the lines in centimetres:

PQ measures 7.5 cm   MN measures 4 cm

1 cm = 5 m   1 cm = 5 cm

∴   7.5 cm = 5 m × 7.5   ∴   4 cm = 5 m × 4

            = 37.5 m   = 20 m

∴   PQ is 37.5 m   ∴   MN is 20 m

Exercise

1. Measure the following lines in centimetres and then, using a scale of 1 cm = 1 m, write down their lengths in metres.

    (a) ————————————————

    (b) ————————

    (c) ——————————————————

    (d) ——————————————

    (e) ————————————————————

2. Measure the following lines in centimetres and then, using a scale of 1 cm = 6 m, write down their lengths in metres.

    (a) ——————————————

    (b) ——————————

    (c) ——————————————————

    (d) ——————————————————

    (e) ——————————————————

3. Measure the following lines in centimetres and then, using a scale of 2 cm = 5 m, write down their lengths in metres.

    (a) ————

    (b) ——————————————————

    (c) ————————————————————————

    (d) ——————————————

    (e) ————————————————————

4. Each figure that follows is drawn to a scale of 1 cm = 2 m. Write down the lengths in metres of the sides asked for.

What are the lengths of AB and BC?

What are the lengths
of LM and LN?

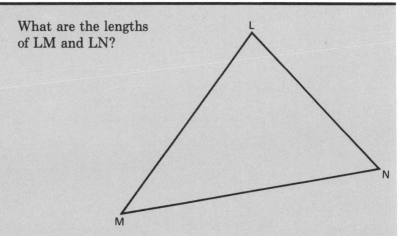

What are the lengths
of PQ, QR, SR and PS?

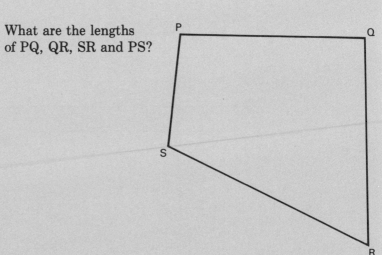

5. The diagram below shows a plan of our lawn and flower
garden drawn to a scale of 1 cm to 10 m.

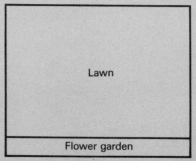

Lawn

Flower garden

(a)   What is the length of the lawn in metres?

(b)   What is the width of the lawn in metres?

(c)   What is the width of the flower garden?

Revision Exercises

Exercise 1 Write the missing number in each pattern:

1. 2,   4,   8,   14,   ...

2. ...,   12,   23,   34,   45

Complete:

3. $(4 \times 10\ 000) + (6 \times 100) + (8 \times 1) = \ ...$

4. $5276 = 5$ thousands $+ \ ...$ hundreds $+ \ 7$ tens $+ \ 6$ ones

5. Write in figures: thirty-five thousand and fifty

6. Write in words: 16 008

7. A farmer has 45 cows. These represent 25 less than the number of pigs he has. How many pigs does the farmer have?

8. If I divided a number by 6, I will get 18 remainder 5. What is this number?

9. Ann has 12 more stamps than Pam and 5 less stamps than Tonya. Tonya has 50 stamps. How many stamps do the three girls have altogether?

10. Ten electric poles are equally spaced along the highway. If any two successive poles are 50 m apart, what is the distance between the first and tenth electric poles?

Exercise 2 **1.** Complete: $3 \times 3 \times 3 \times \ ... \ = 54$

2. Find the lowest common multiple of 6 and 9.

3. Which of these is *not* a multiple of 8? (4, 8, 32, 56)

4. Which factor of 18 is missing from here?
(1, 2, 3, 6, 18, . . .)

5. Pick out the *prime number* from this set of numbers:
(21, 23, 25, 27)

Use the following digits (2, 3, 6, 4) once only in each question
to write:

6. the smallest possible even number

7. the largest possible even number

8. the smallest possible odd number.

9. The sum of 3 consecutive numbers is 42. Which of these is
the smallest?

10. Find the sum of 5 consecutive odd numbers if the biggest
of them is 17.

Exercise 3   Complete:

1. $\dfrac{}{5} = \dfrac{12}{20}$ **3.** $\dfrac{3}{10} + \dfrac{2}{5} = \dfrac{}{10}$ **5.** $\dfrac{5}{8} \times \dfrac{1}{5} = \ldots$

2. $\dfrac{4}{3} = \dfrac{}{12}$ **4.** $\dfrac{11}{3} - \dfrac{3}{4} = \dfrac{}{12}$ **6.** $\dfrac{1}{2} \div \dfrac{3}{4} = \ldots$

7. What is $\frac{3}{4}$ of 48?

8. Arrange these fractions in order of size, beginning with
the smallest first: $\frac{3}{8}$, $\frac{1}{2}$, $\frac{2}{3}$, $\frac{5}{12}$.

9. $\frac{2}{3}$ of the pupils in a class took part in the mathematics
quiz. If 24 pupils took part in the mathematics quiz, how
many pupils were in the class?

10. A tank of $\frac{2}{5}$ full of water holds 40 litres. How many litres of
water would it take to fill the tank?

Exercise 4   Write the answer for:

1. $2.04 + 3.6 + 4$ **3.** 1.29×0.03

2. $5.7 - 0.57$ **4.** $4.2 \div 0.03$

5. Complete: $0.009 = \dfrac{9}{-}$

6. What is $\frac{3}{5}$ written as a decimal?

7. Arrange these decimals in order of size, beginning with the smallest first: 0.4,   0.12,   0.3,   0.25.

In the number 45.26, the value of:

8. the 5 = 5 **. . .**

9. the 2 = 2 **. . .**

10. Tony ran the 100 m race in 13.2 s. Ryan ran the same race 0.4 s faster than Tony. What was Ryan's time for the race?

Exercise 5 Complete:

1. $\dfrac{16}{40} = \ldots\%$

2. $45\% = \dfrac{9}{\underline{}}$

3. Express 12 as a percentage of 20.

In a test, 68% of the pupils passed, 18% got distinctions and the others failed.

4. What percentage of the pupils failed?

5. How many pupils failed?

The figure to the right shows a cube:

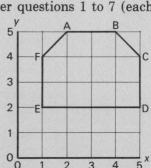

6. How many faces has the cube?

7. How many corners has the cube?

8. How many edges has the cube?

9. What shape is each face of the cube, a square, rectangle or circle?

10. How many right angles are in this cube?

Exercise 6 Study this diagram and then answer questions 1 to 7 (each square is 1 cm by 1 cm):

1. Name a line parallel to AB.

2. Name a perpendicular line.

3. Name a horizontal line.

4. How many right angles are formed with the sides of ABCDEF?

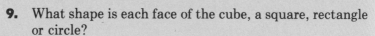
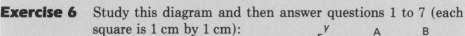
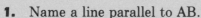

5. What is the area of this figure?

6. What are the coordinates of A?

7. Which point has coordinates (4, 5)?

8. What is the value of a?   **9.** What is the value of c?

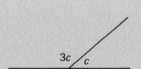

10. The diameter of a circle is 15 cm. What is the measurement of its radius?

Exercise 7 Complete:

1. $16 - n = 4$ **2.** $\dfrac{24}{n} = 6$

$\therefore \quad n = \ldots$ $\therefore n = \ldots$

3. What number when multiplied by itself gives 64?

4. The perimeter of this shape is 32 cm. Find the measurement of the sides marked a.

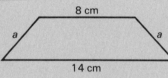

5. Find the area of this shape.

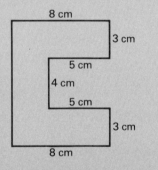

6. 5 times a certain number is 60. What is the number?

7. 6 similar ballpoint pens cost $15. Find the cost of 8 of these ballpoint pens.

8. The price of a ruler is 65 ¢. A notebook costs three times as much as a ruler. Find the total cost of 2 similar rulers and 2 similar notebooks.

9. What number must be taken from the sum of 34 and 29 to give 48?

10. The average attendance of a class of pupils for the first 4 days of a week was 23. How many pupils need to attend class on the fifth day to increase the average to 25?

Exercise 8

1. 5 boys shared $125.25 equally. How much does each boy receive?

2. Given that US $1.00 = BB $1.98, how much in BB currency would you get for US $50.00?

3. Which bag is heavier, a bag containing a packet weighing 3 kg or a similar bag containing 8 packets each weighing 400 g?

4. 4 athletes completed a road race in a total time of 5 h and 12 min. What was their average time for the race?

5. Toni has 45 pictures and Akari has 67 pictures. How many pictures must Akari give Toni so that both of them have the same number of pictures?

Tasha picked three times as many cherries as Ankar. Together they picked 72 cherries.

6. How many cherries did Ankar pick?

7. How many cherries did Tasha pick?

8. A length of rope is 75 m long. It is cut into two pieces so that one piece is 9 m longer than the other piece. What is the measurement of the longer piece?

9. A clock loses 3 min every hour. If it is put right at 8.00 a.m. on Sunday, what time will it read when the correct time is 12.00 noon the same Sunday?

10. A cyclist rode from home to the stadium at 20 km per hour and took 15 min. How far from the stadium did the cyclist live?